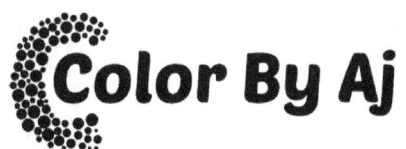

MINDFUL mandalas

Relaxing Adult Coloring Book Volume 1 - Improved Edition

FREE YOUR CREATIVITY !

FREE YOUR IMAGINATION !

Adult Coloring Book with
30 Mindful Mandala Designs to Color
ISBN: 9798653644085

By AJBailey
Copyright © 2020 AJ Bailey. All rights reserved
No part of this book can be reproduced in any form without the
written permission for the copyright holder.

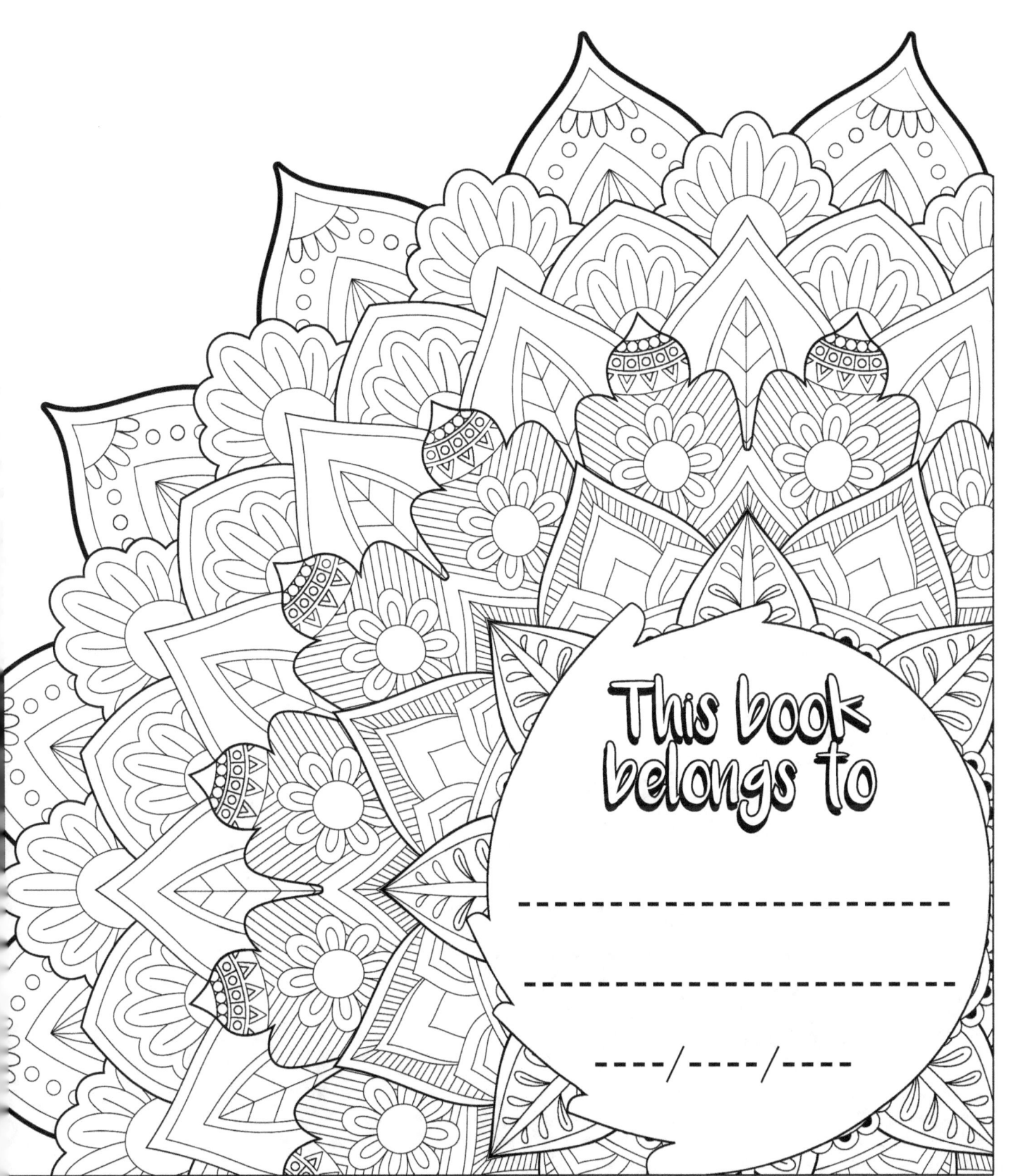

About this book

Thank you for grabbing a copy of my Mindful Mandala Coloring Book Vol 1.

This new and improved version has a mixture of better line work and enhanced designs.

This book encourages you to use your imagination to create vibrant patterns that reveal your hidden creative potential and bring you closer to your true self.

In this book there are 30 amazing Mandala designs ready for you to color. These designs vary from easy to detailed but each is designed to bring you joy and hopefully challenge your coloring skills.

You can use colored pencils of any type. But if you would like to use gel pens, wet medium, markers and so on, there is a separate page at the back of this book for you to cut out and place behind the page you are coloring to help stop any bleed through on the image below.

I would like to see your final creations so please head on over to my website and send me your images.

www.ColorByAj.com

FREE COLORING PAGES
visit https://www.colorbyaj.com/free-coloring-pages

So thanks again for your support and enjoy the book.

-AJ

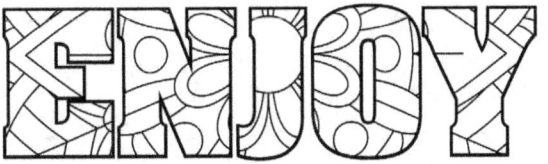

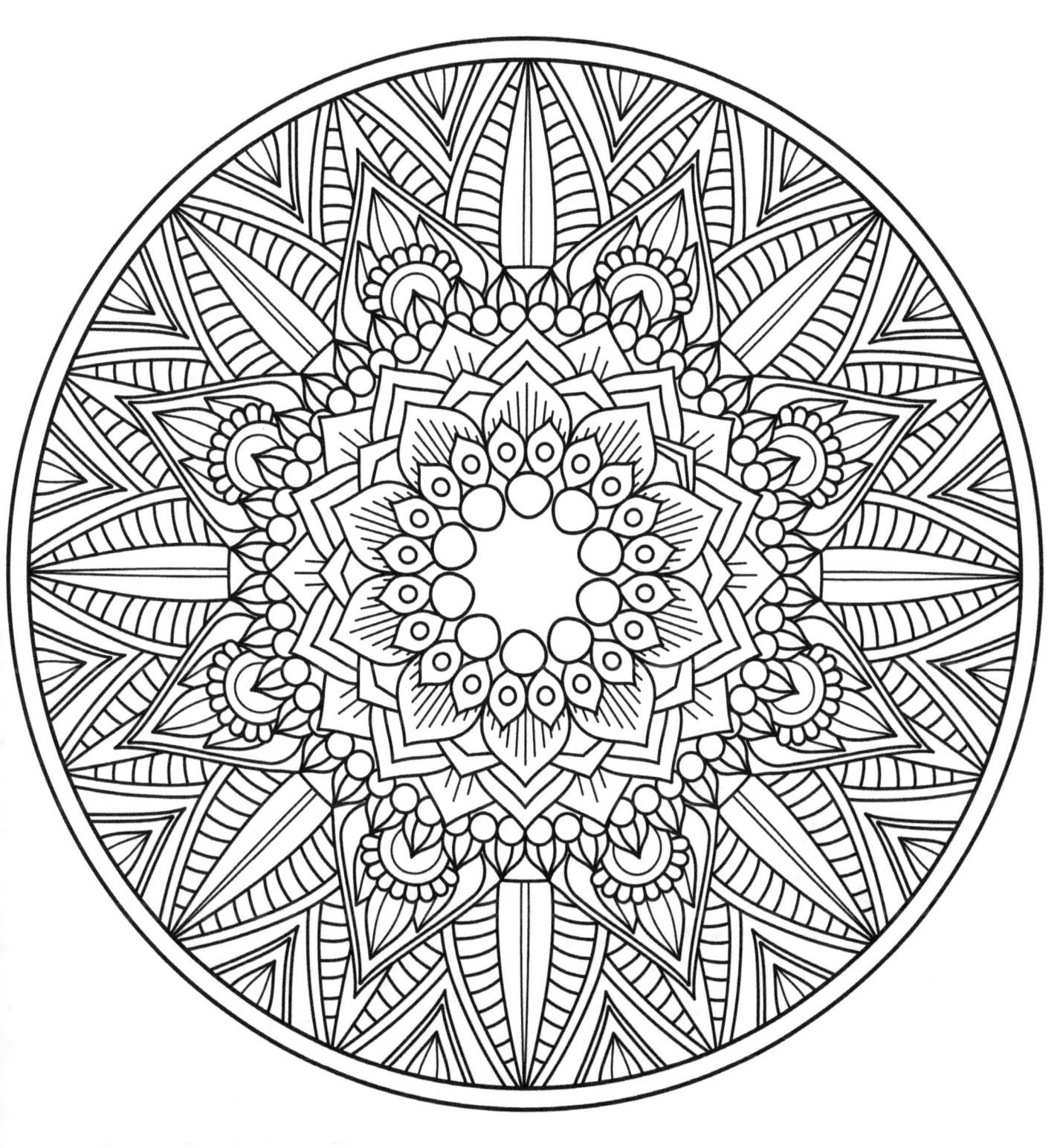

___/___/___

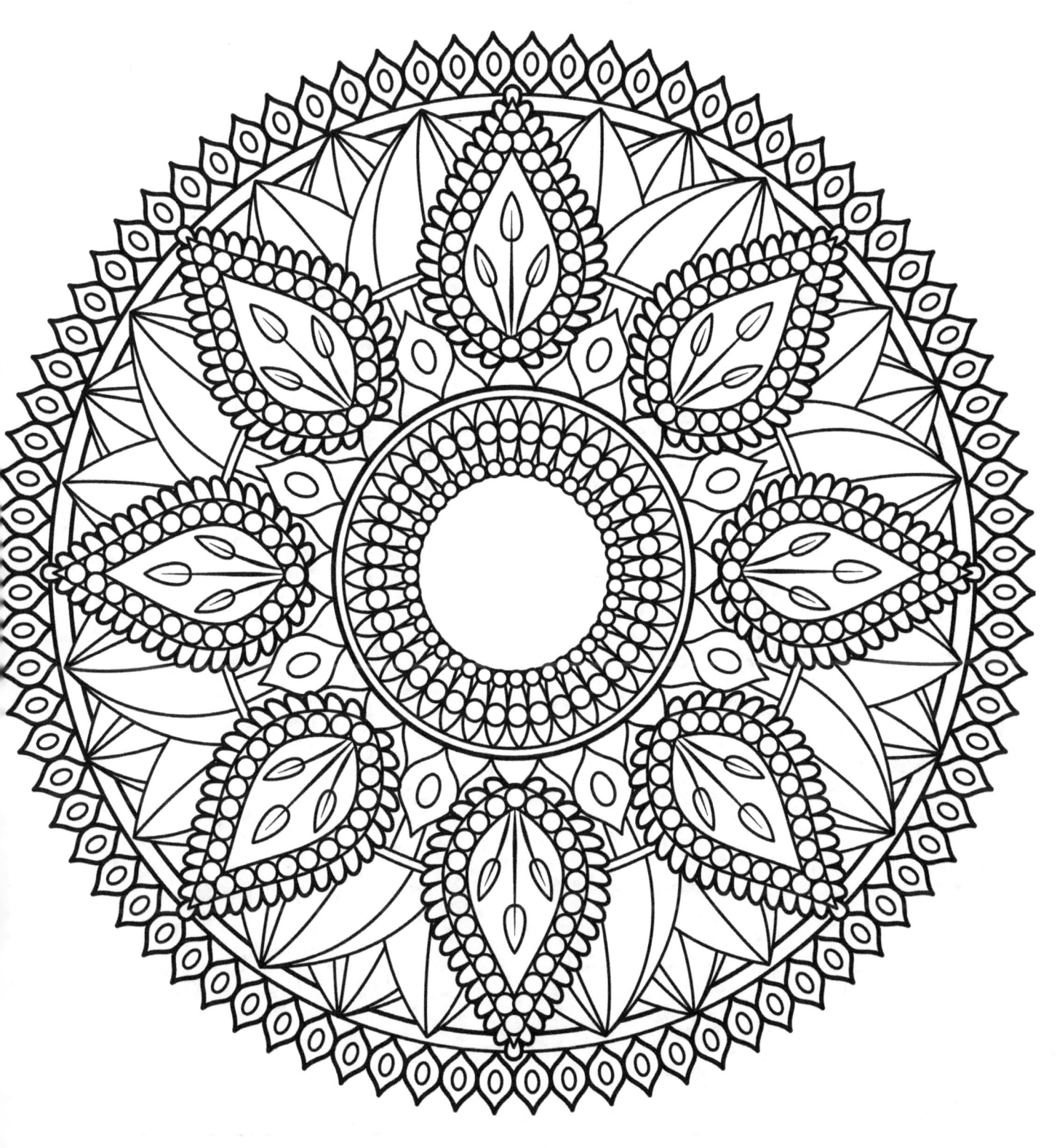

_____

___ / ___ / ___

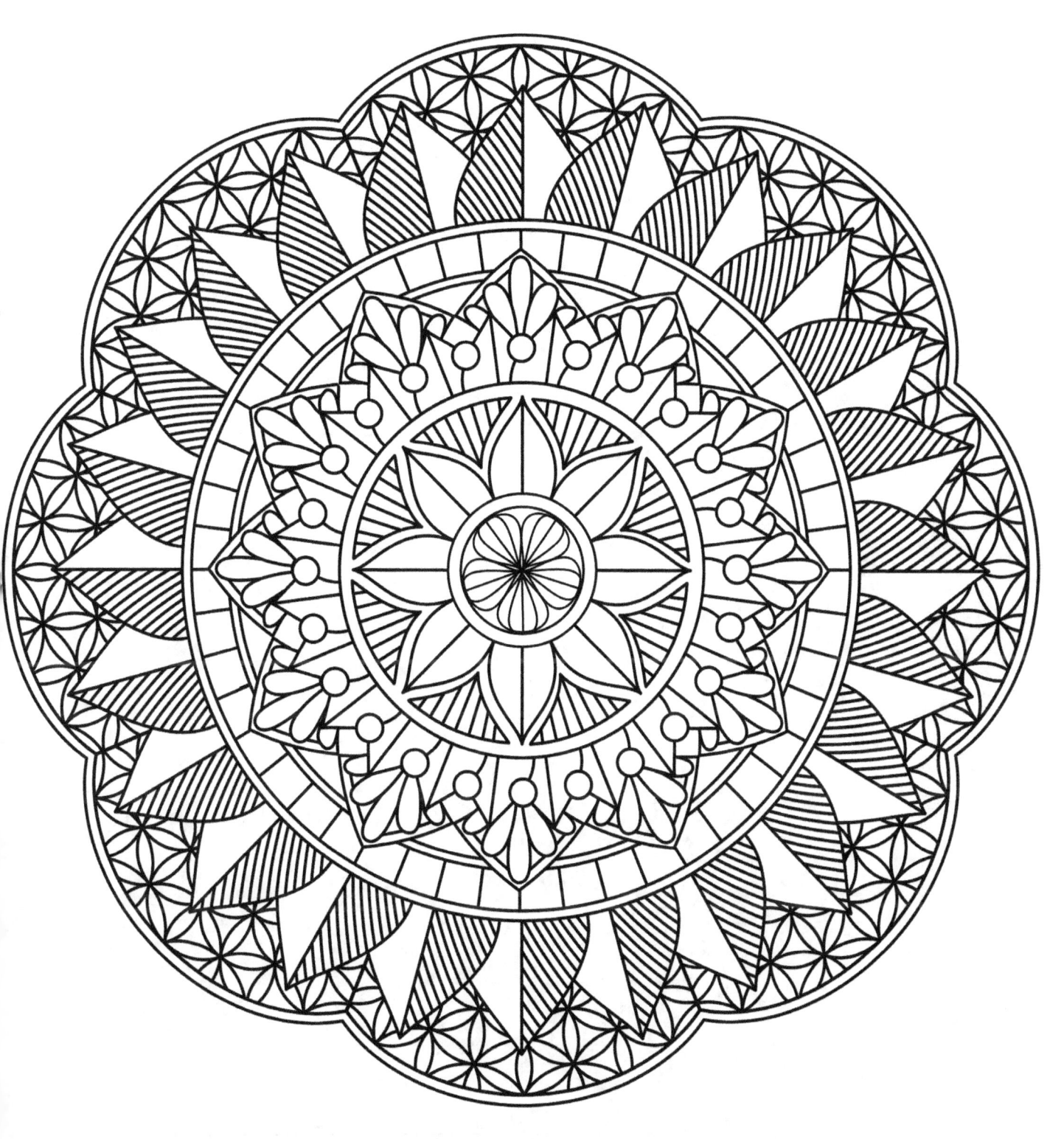

_____

——/——/——

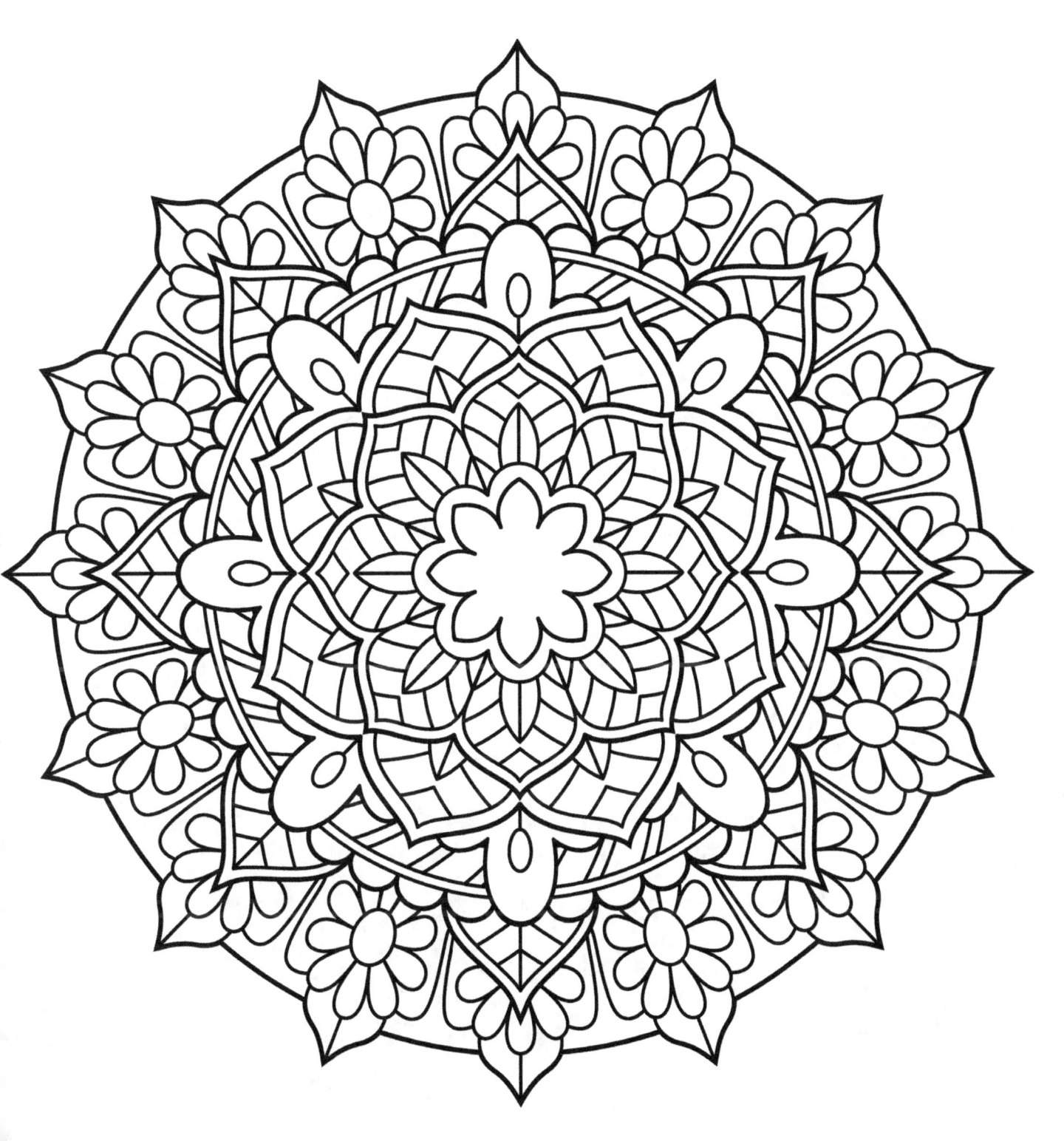

_____

___ / ___ / ___

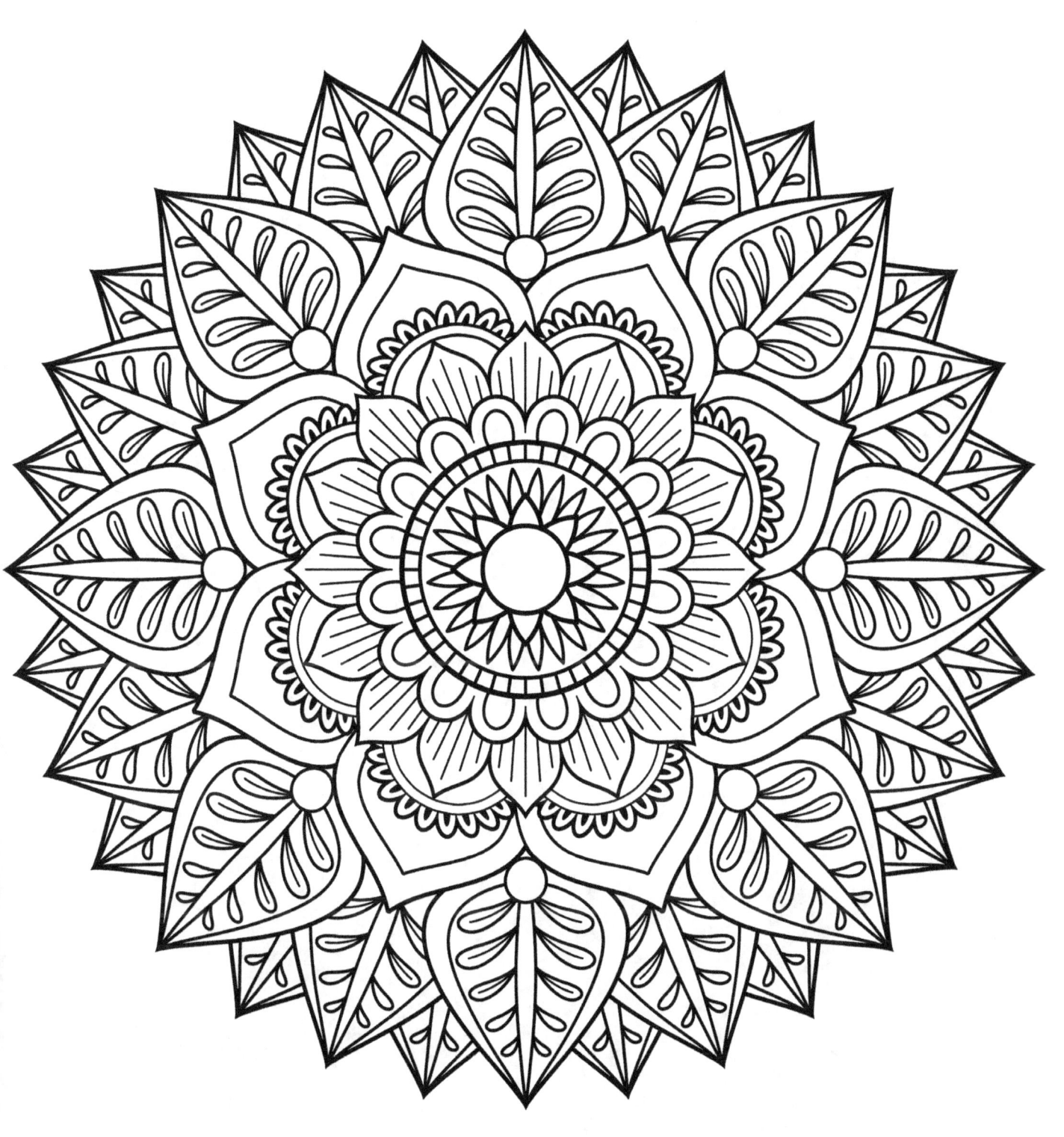

_____

___ / ___ / ___

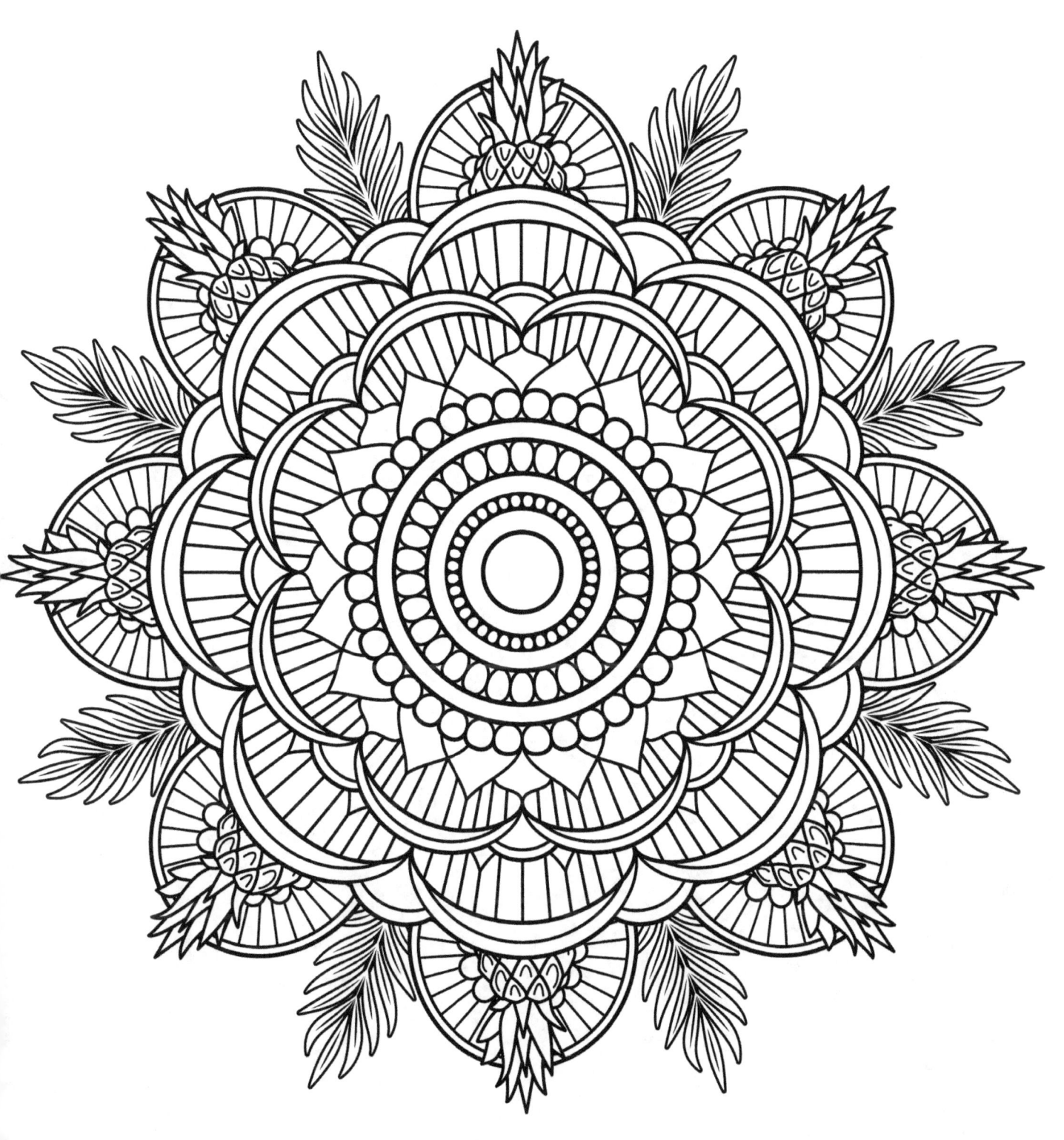

_____

___ / ___ / ___

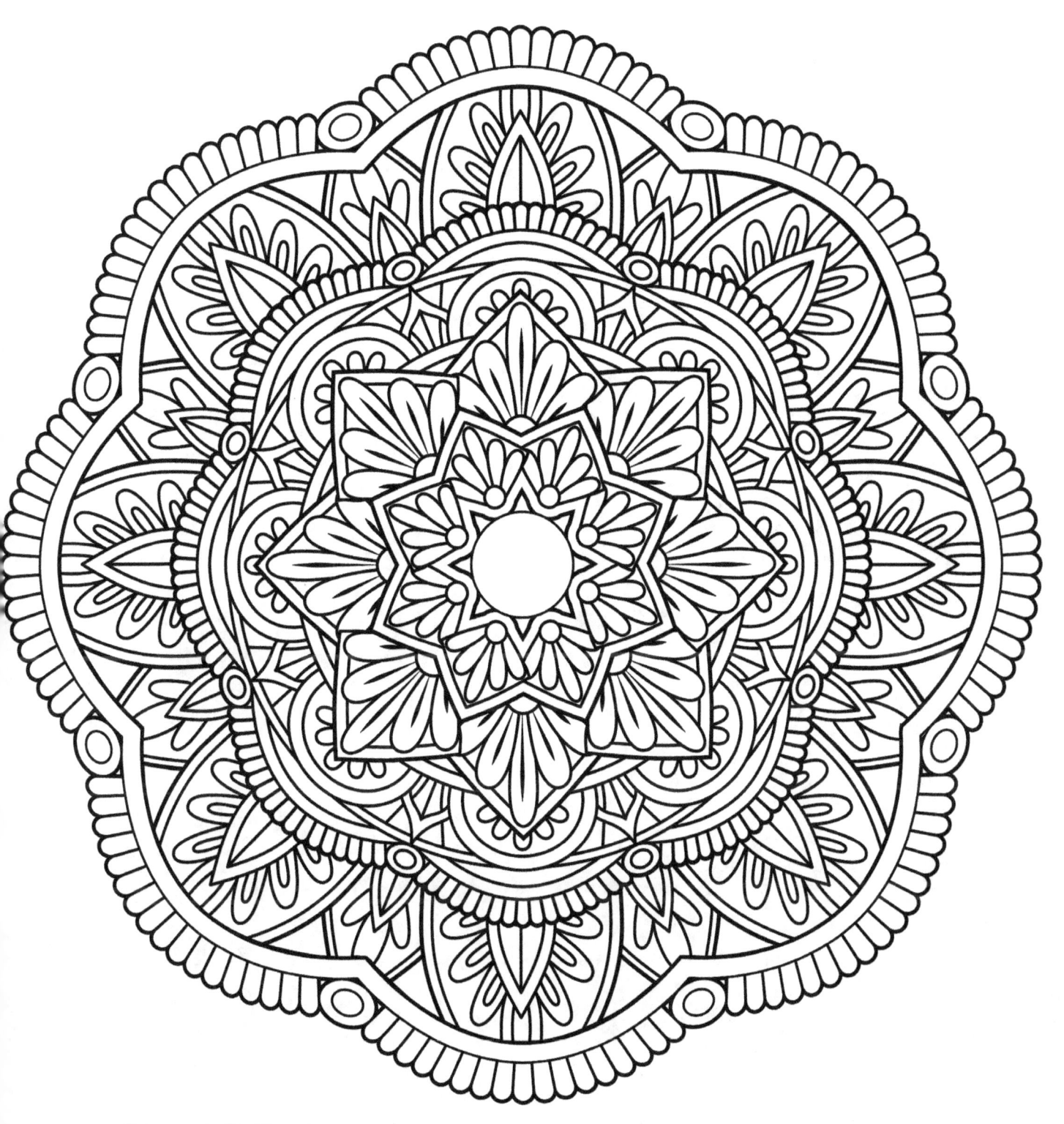

_____

___ / ___ / ___

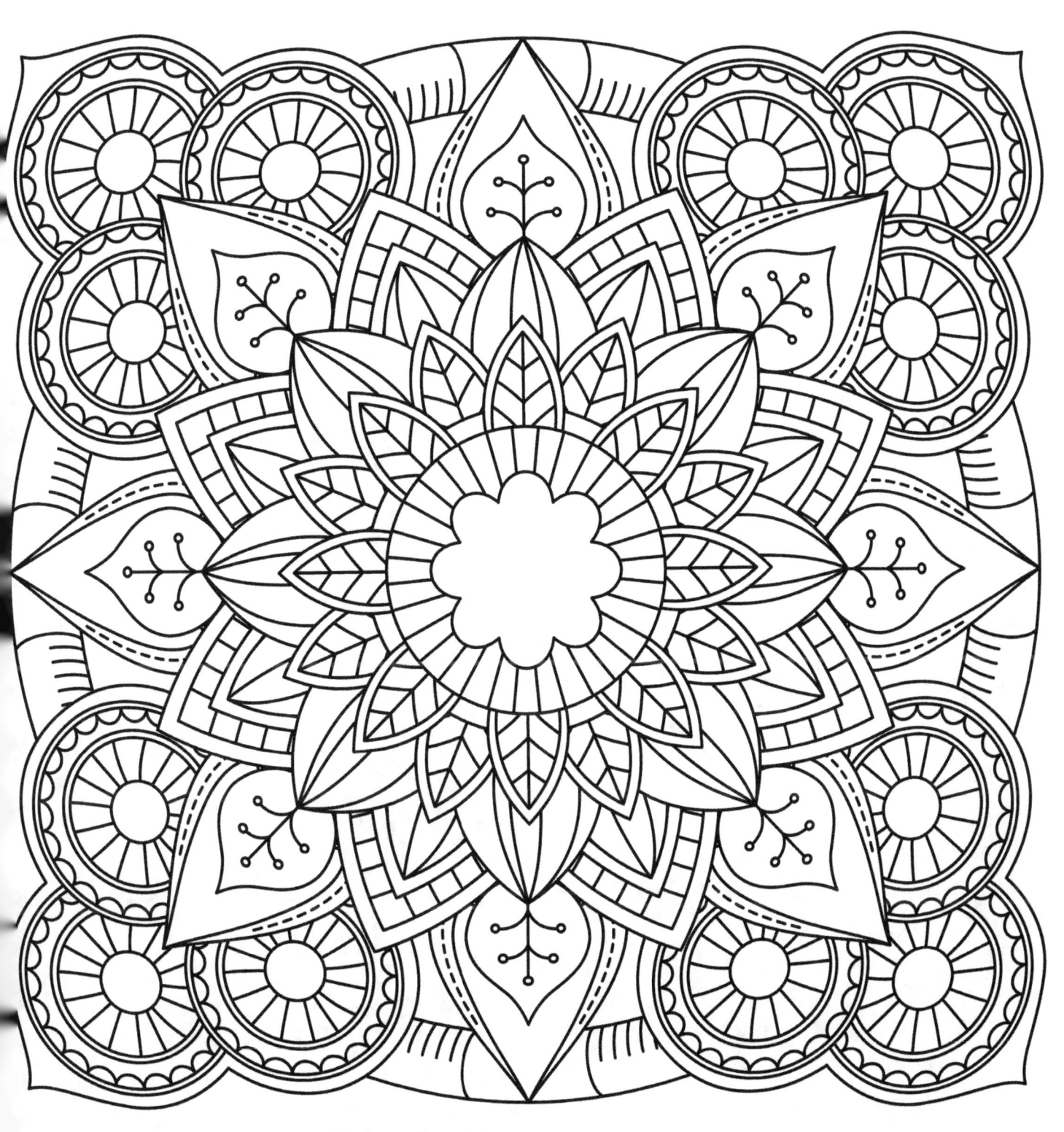

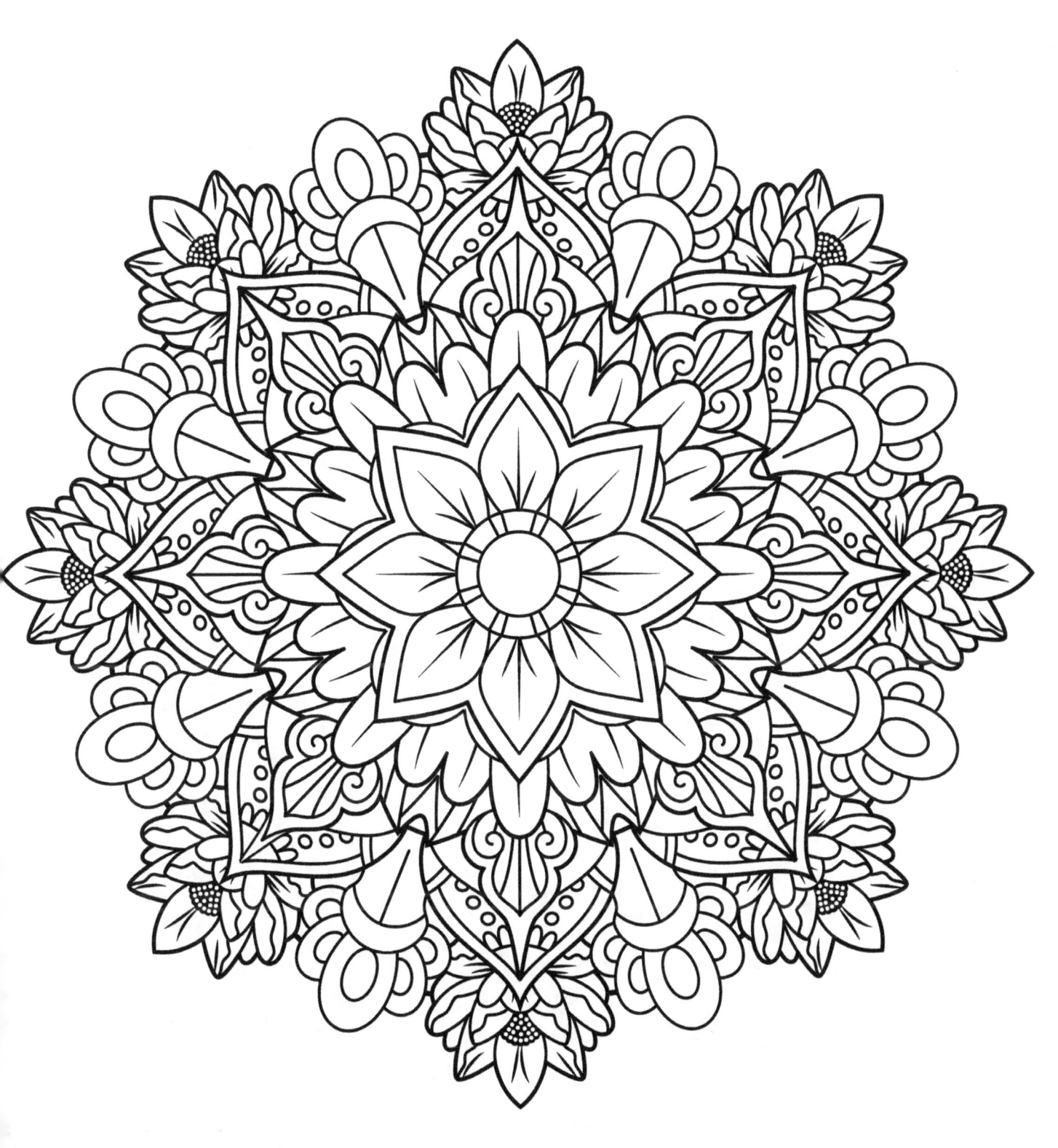

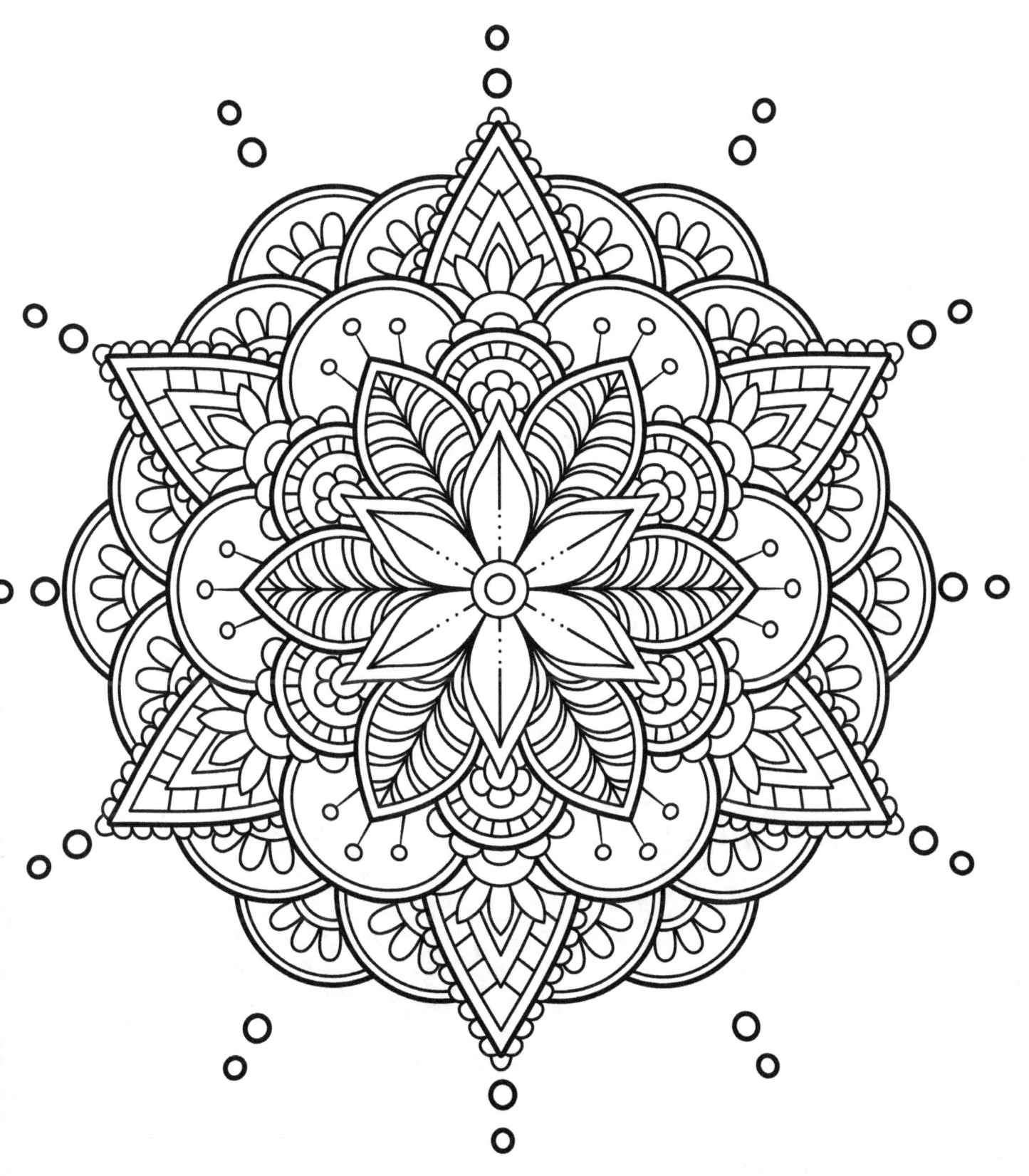

_____

___ / ___ / ___

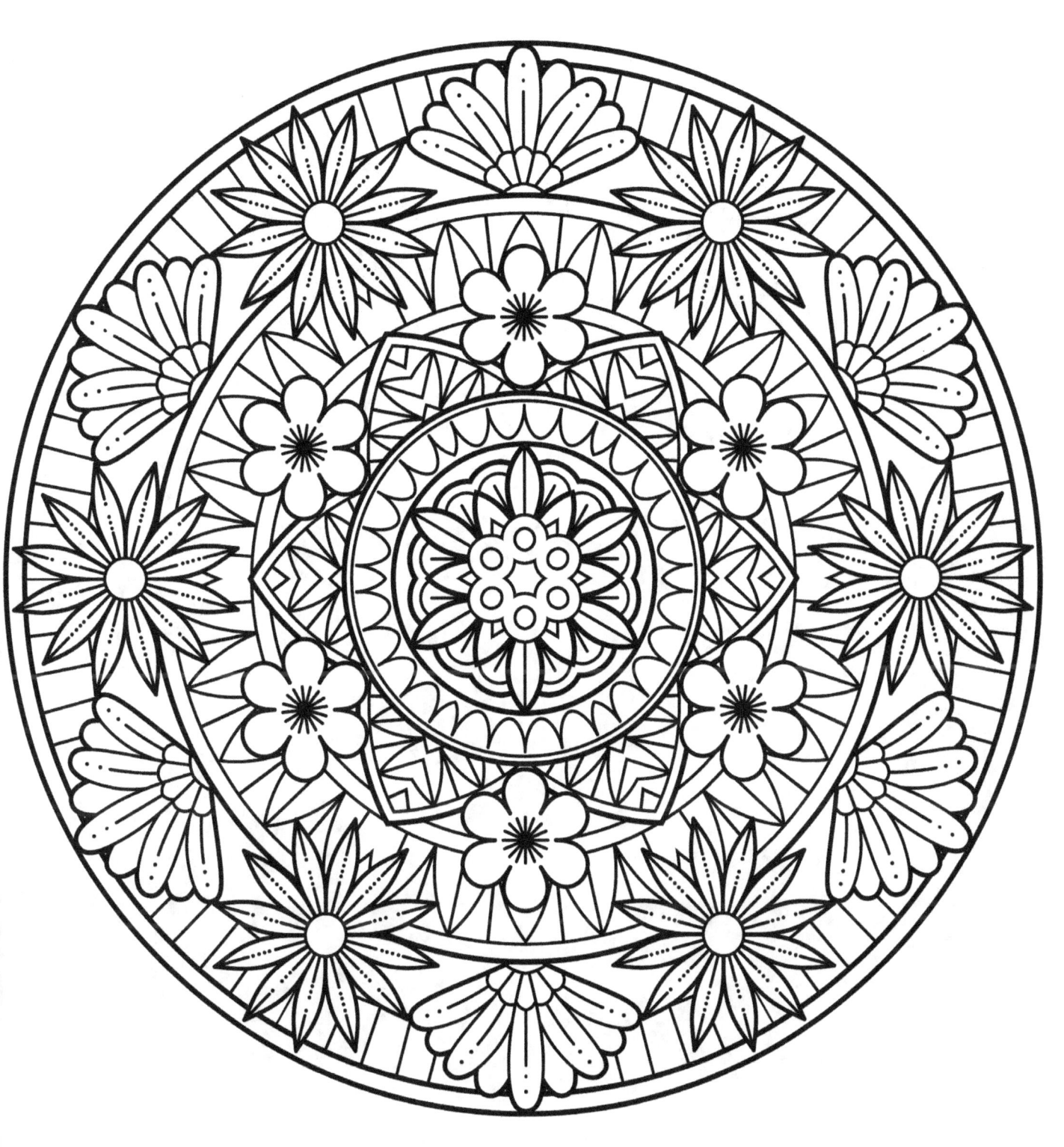

_____

___ / ___ / ___

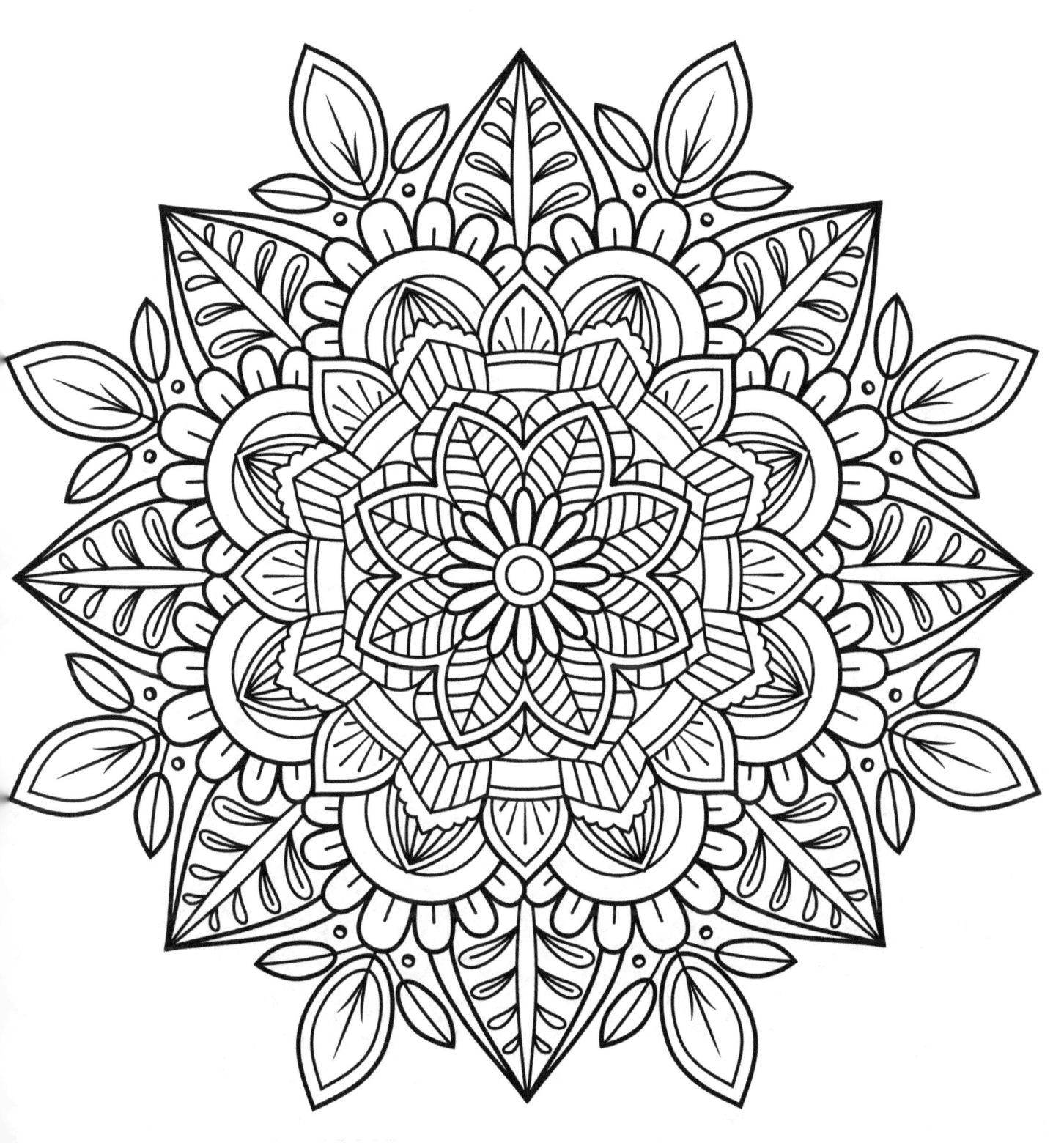

_____

___/___/___

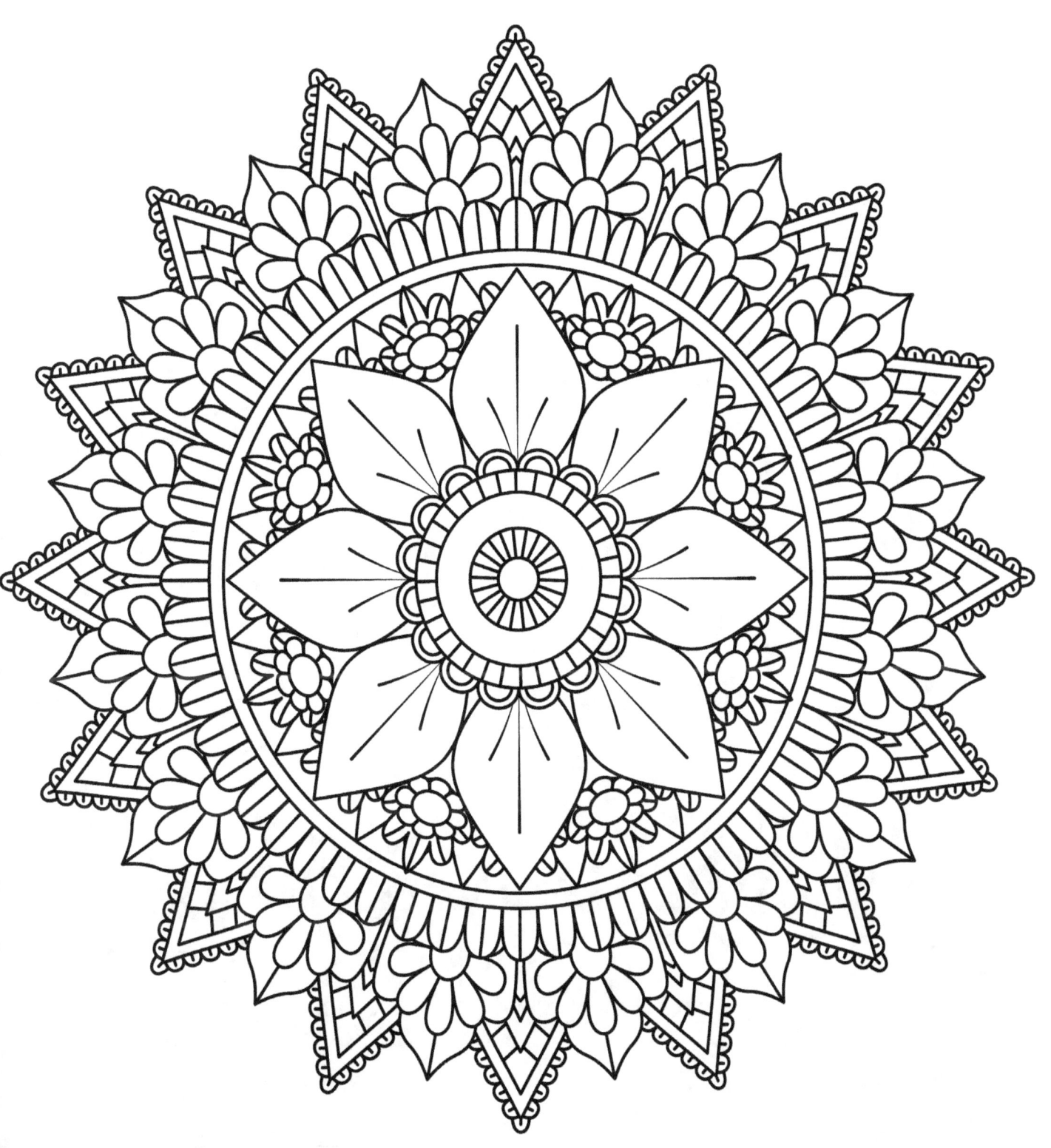

_____

___ / ___ / ___

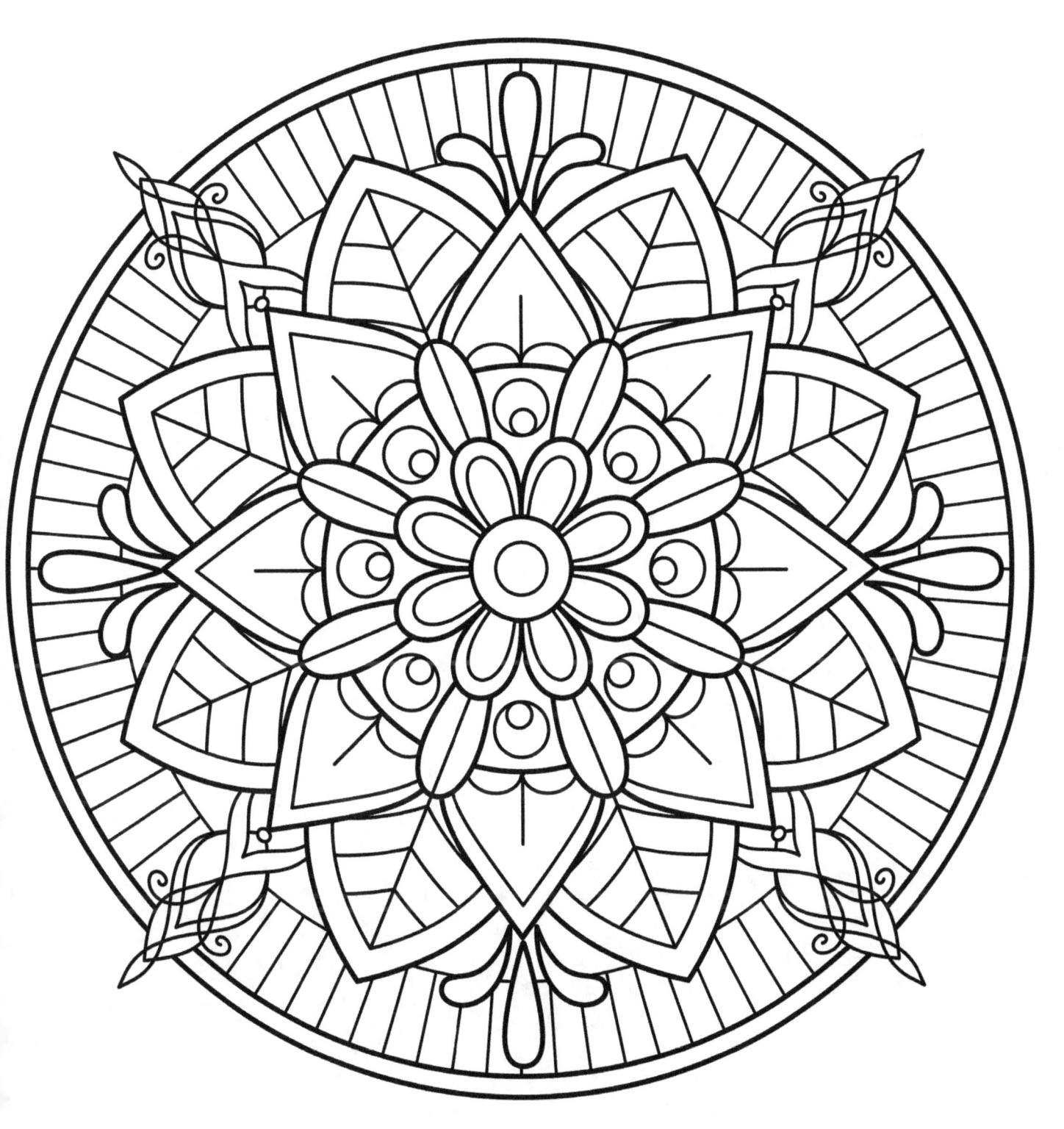

___/___/___

___/___/___

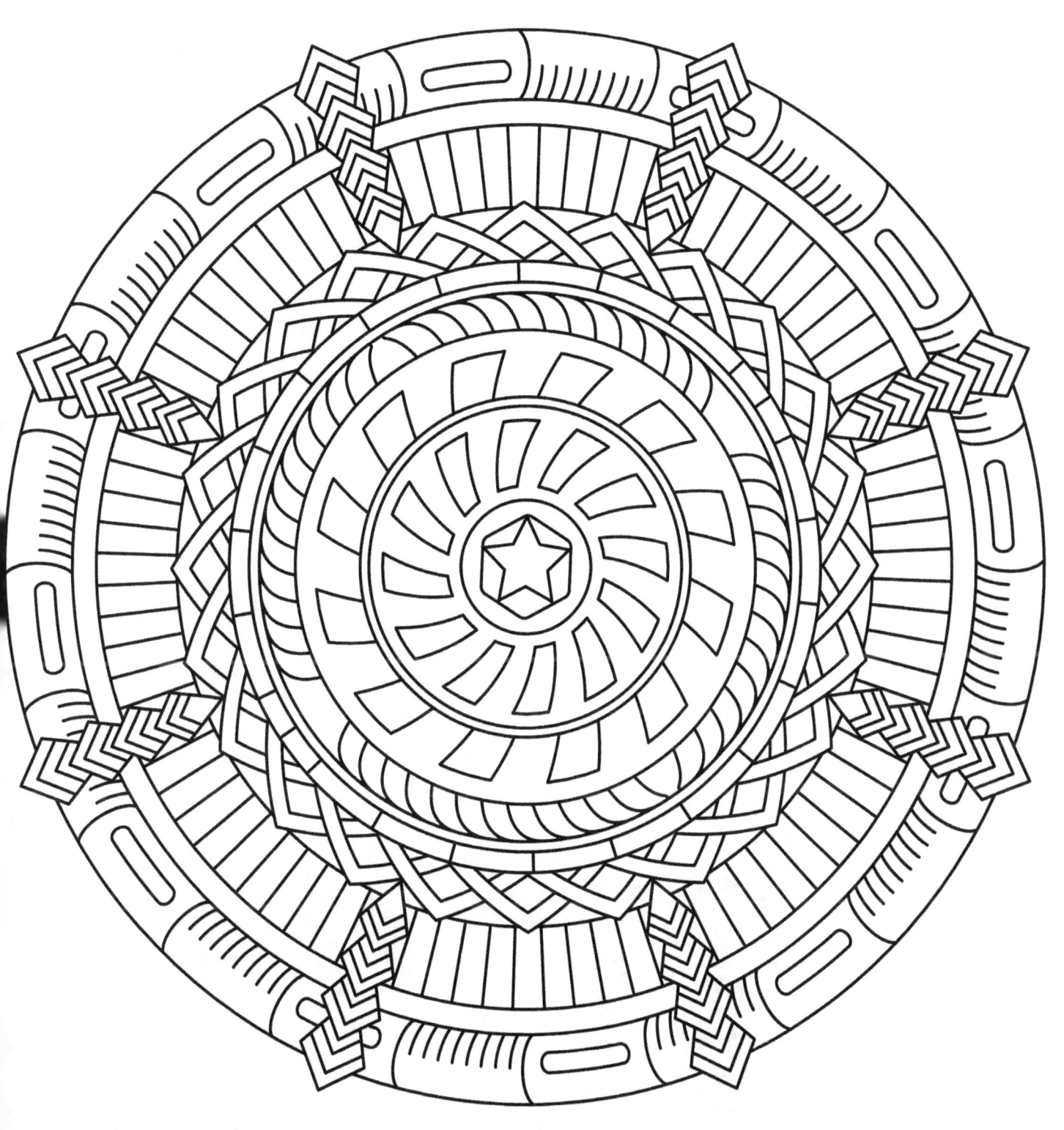

_____

___ / ___ / ___

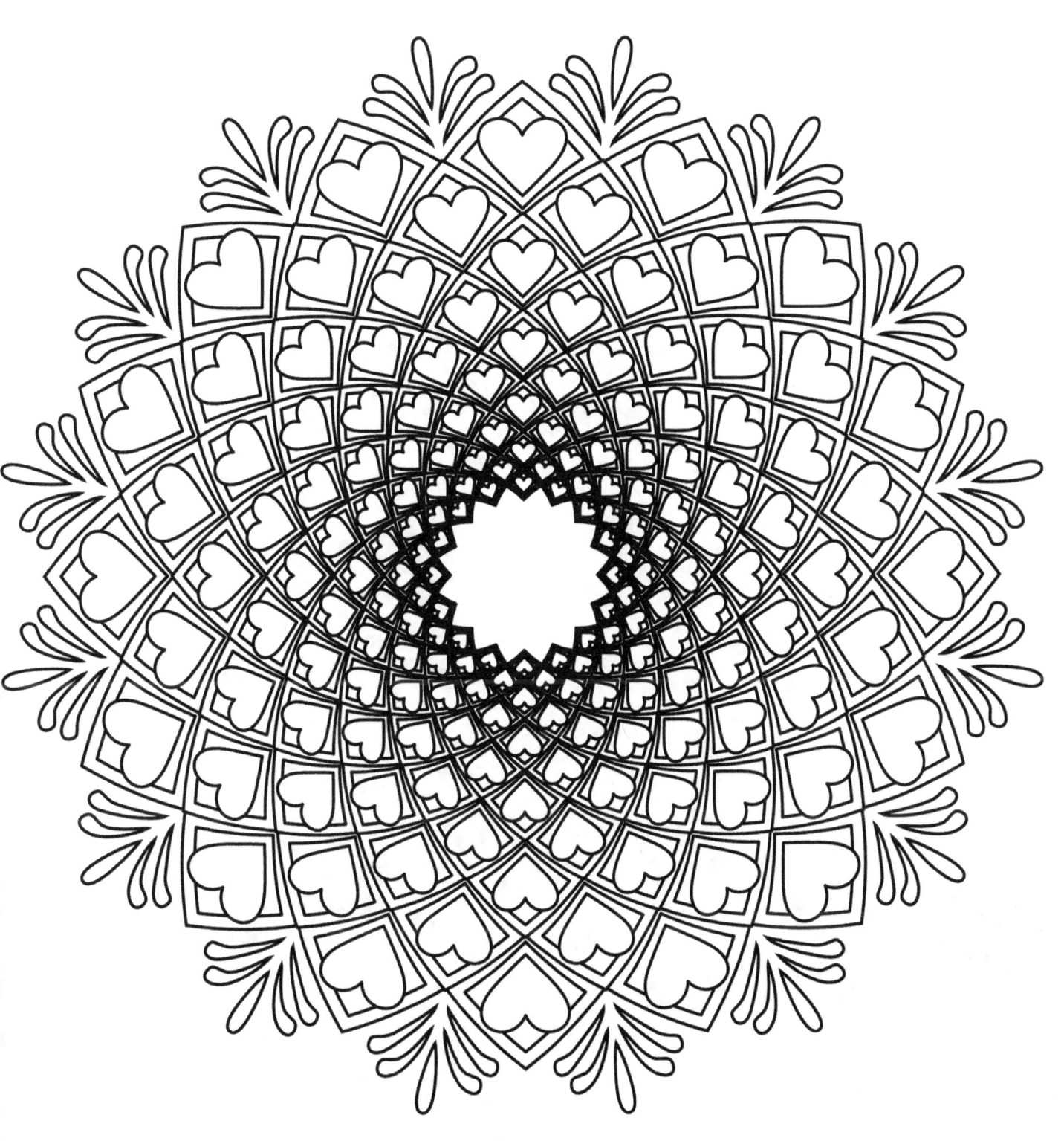

___/___/___

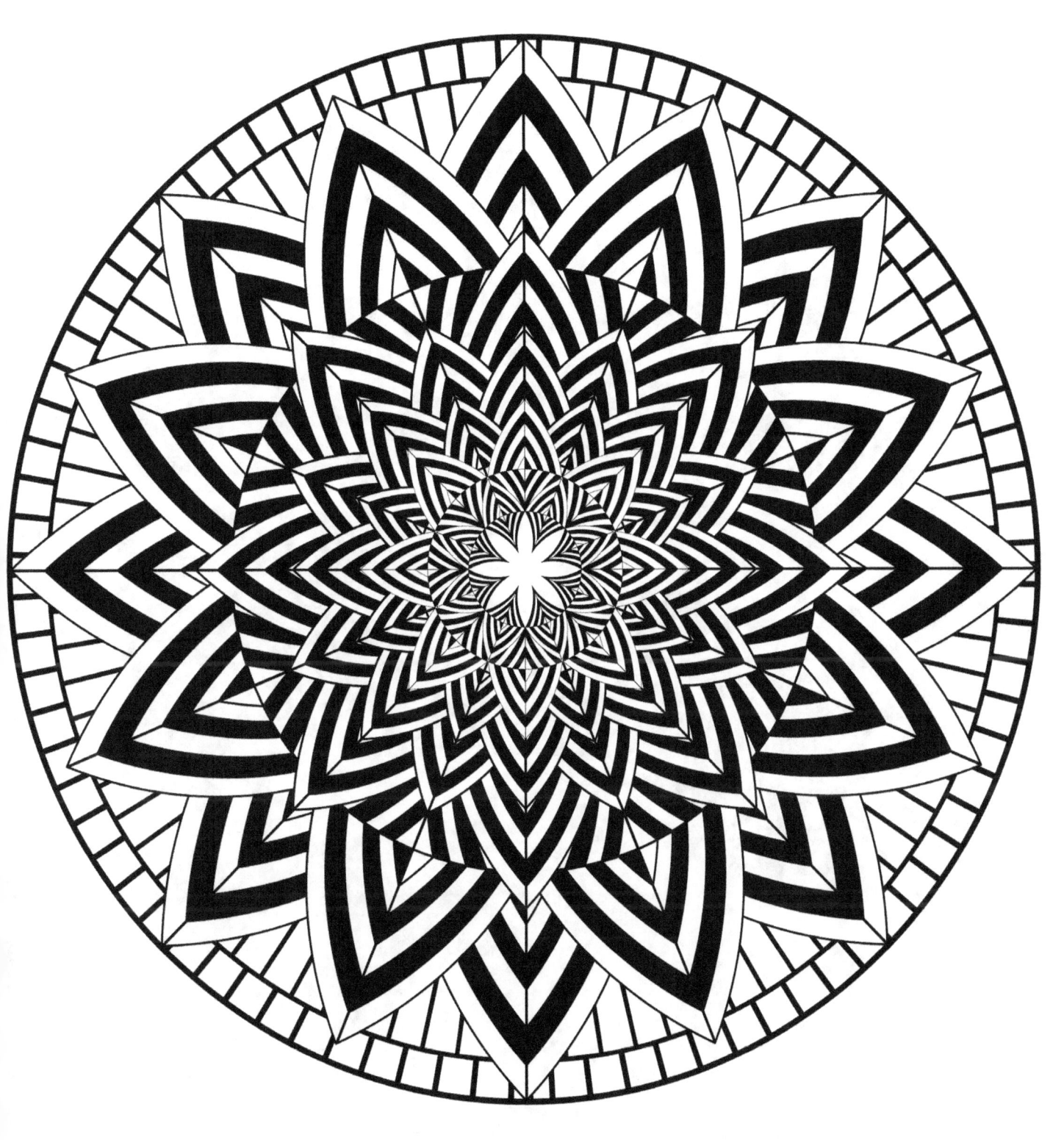

_____

___ / ___ / ___

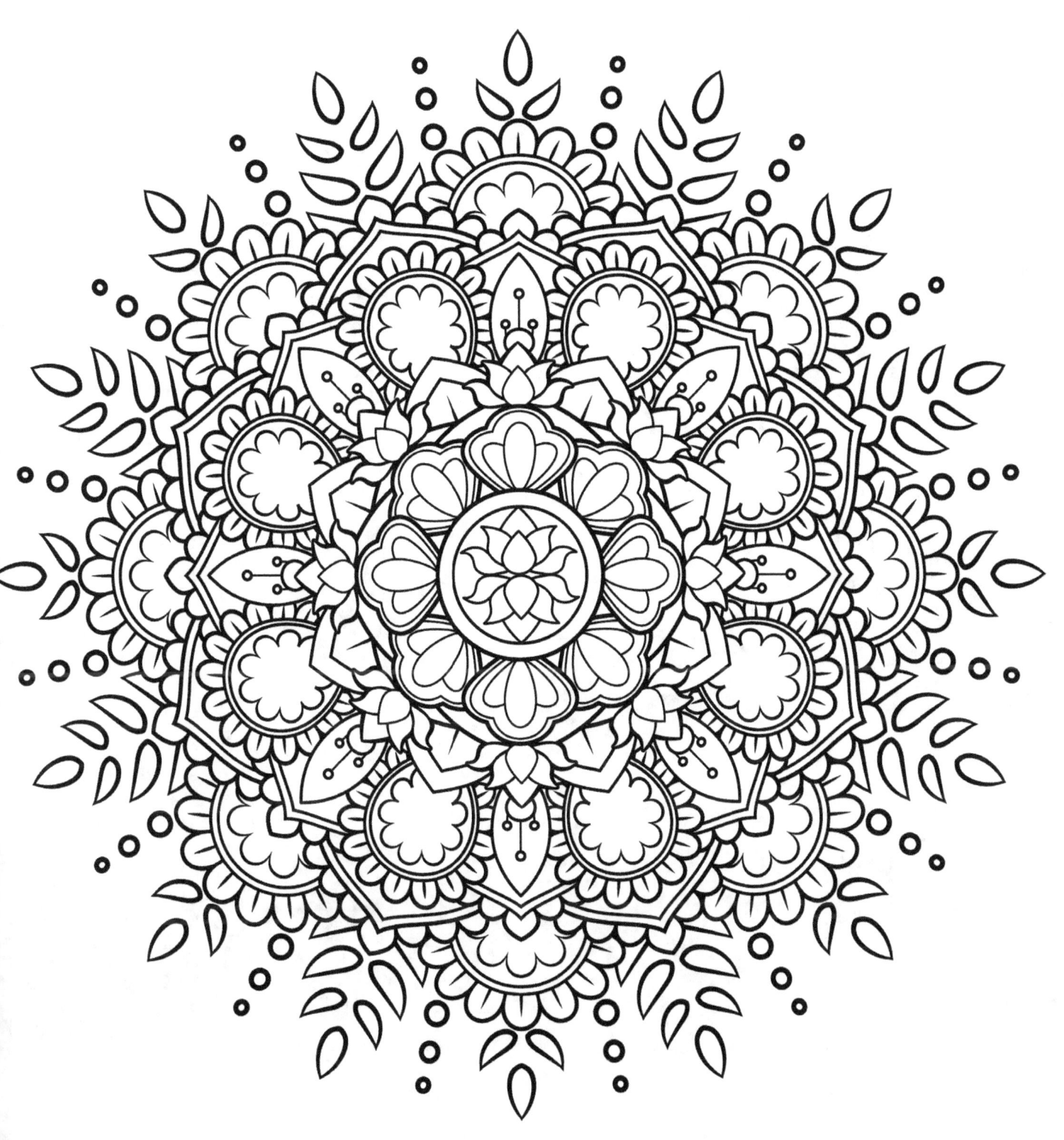

_____

___ / ___ / ___

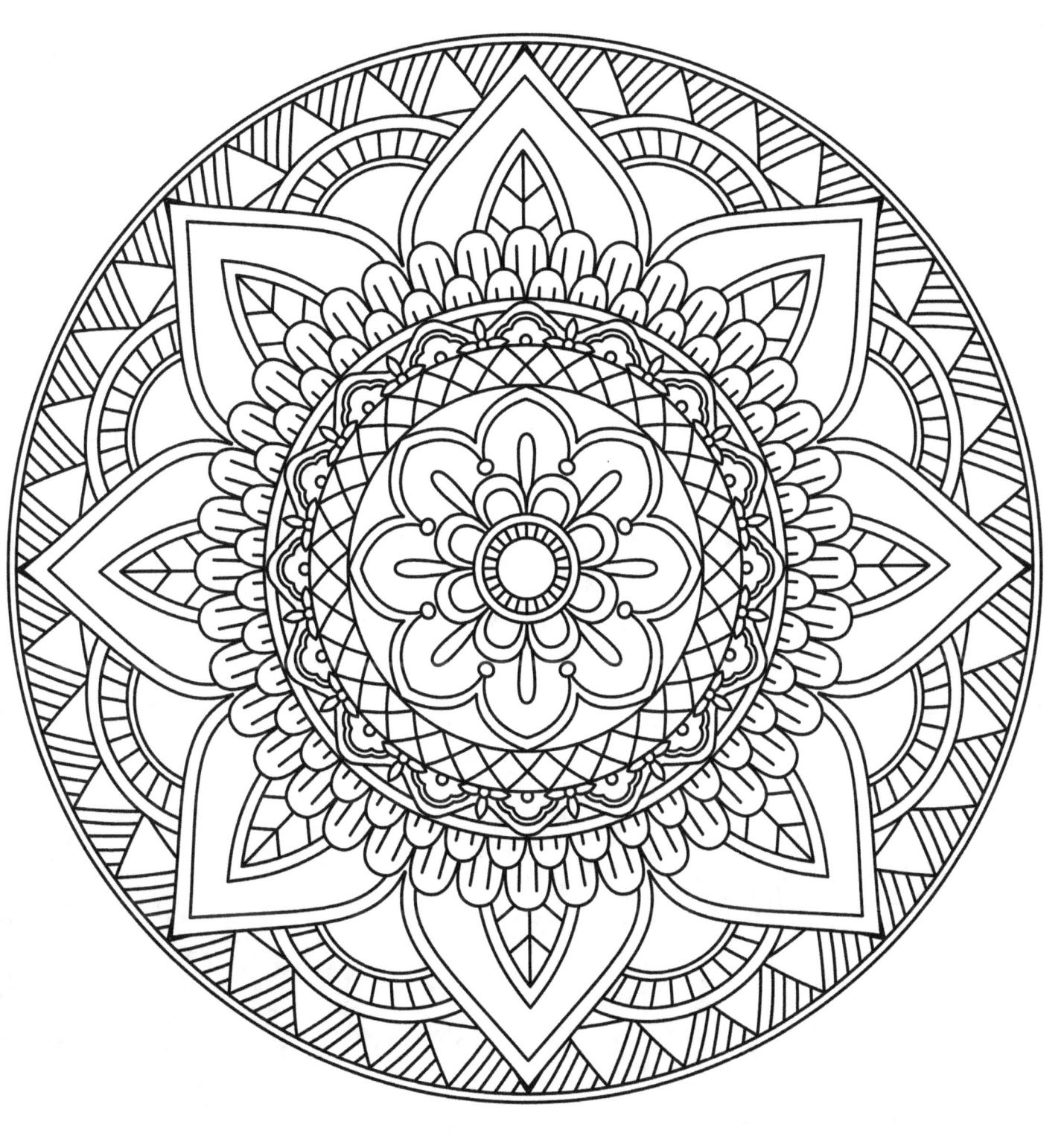

_____

___ / ___ / ___

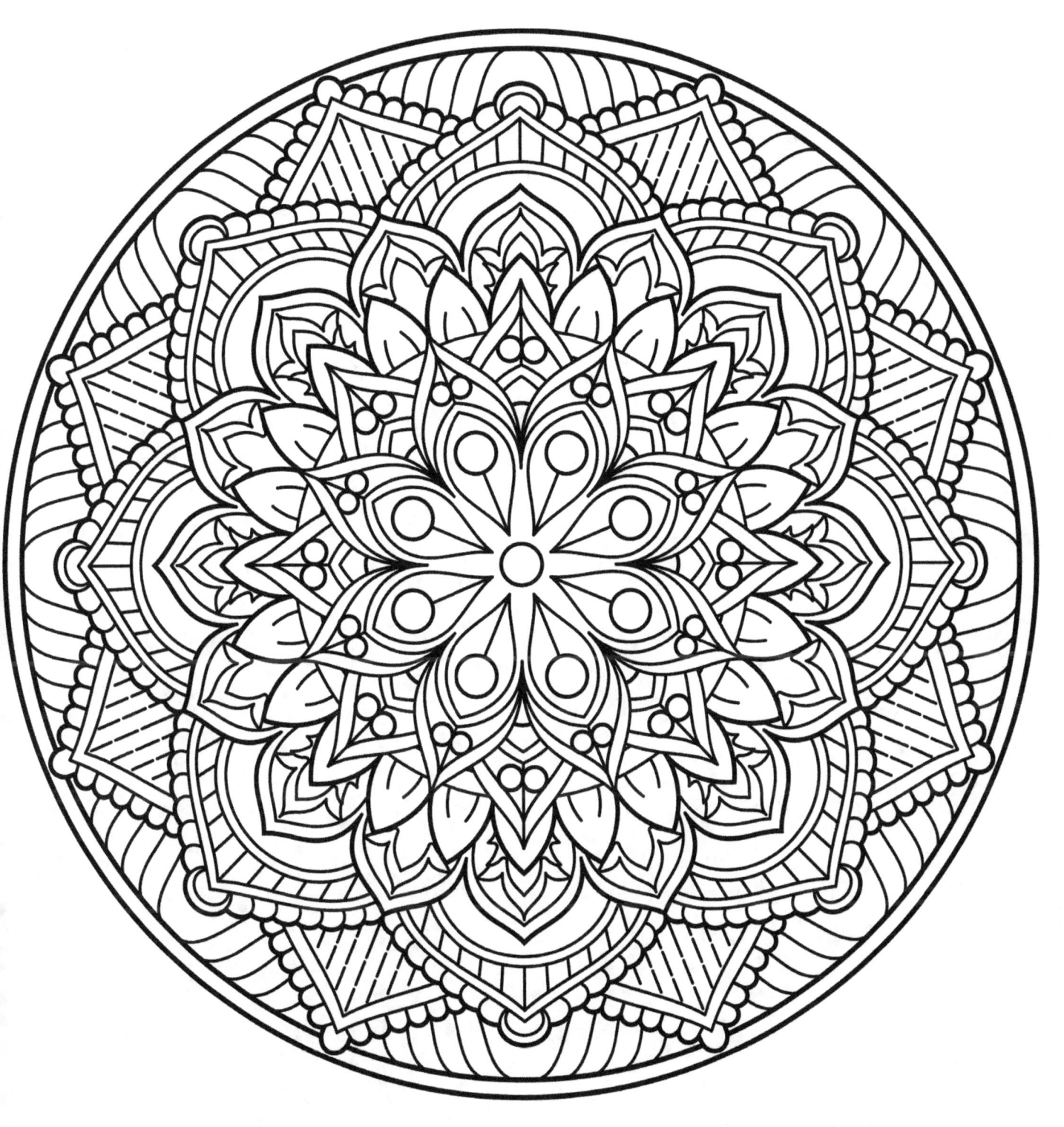

_____

___ / ___ / ___

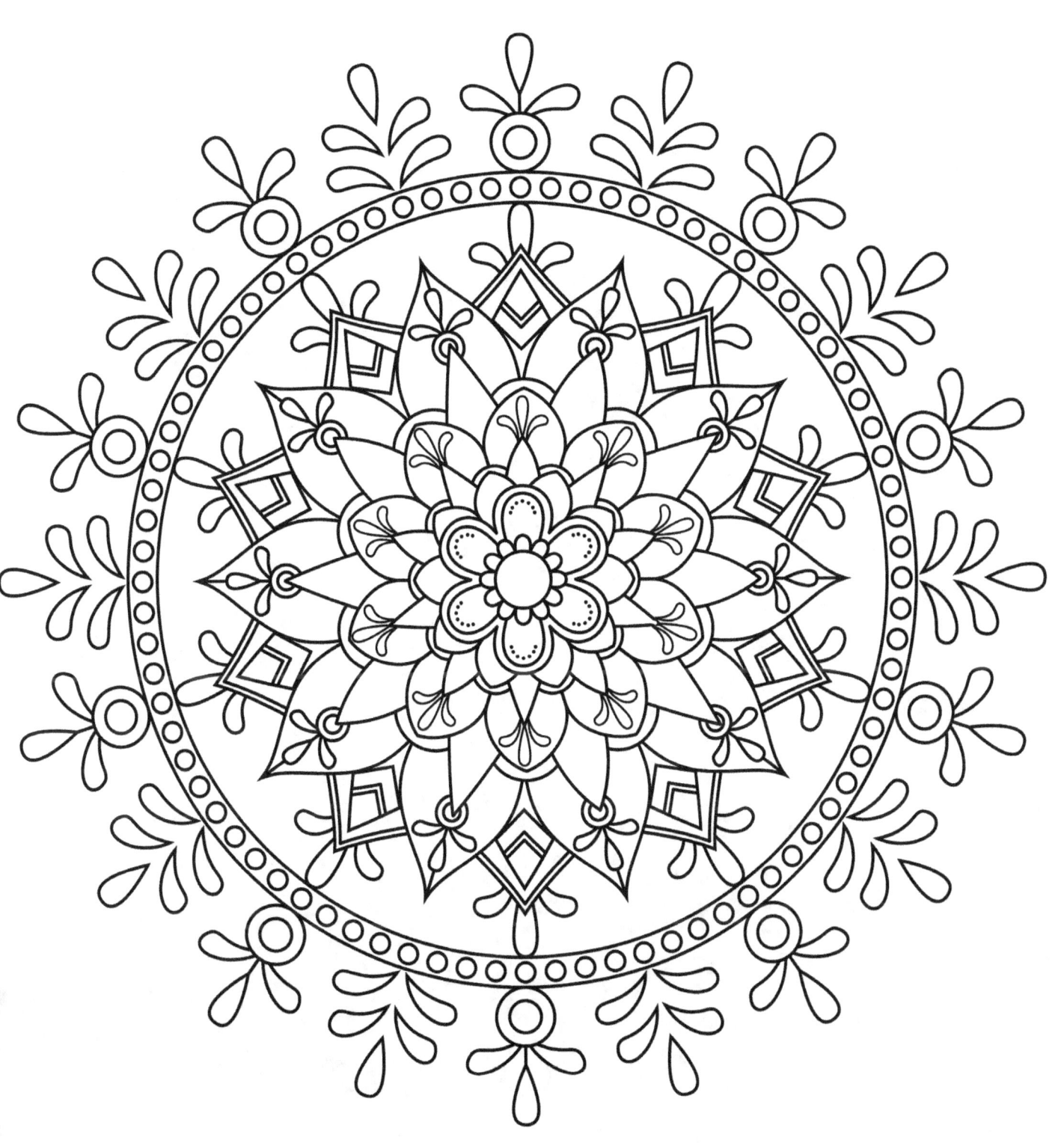

_____

___ / ___ / ___

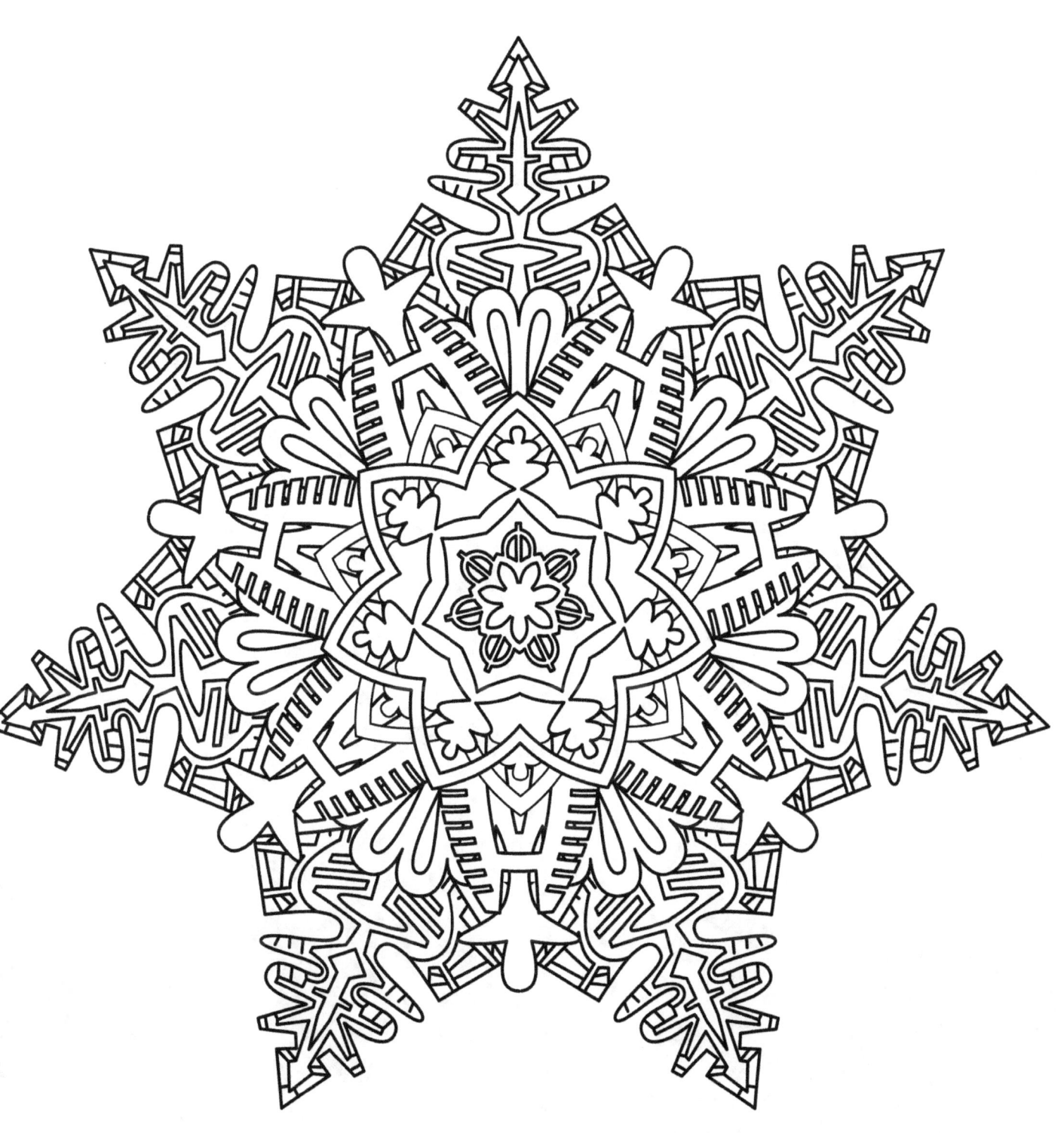

_____

___ / ___ / ___

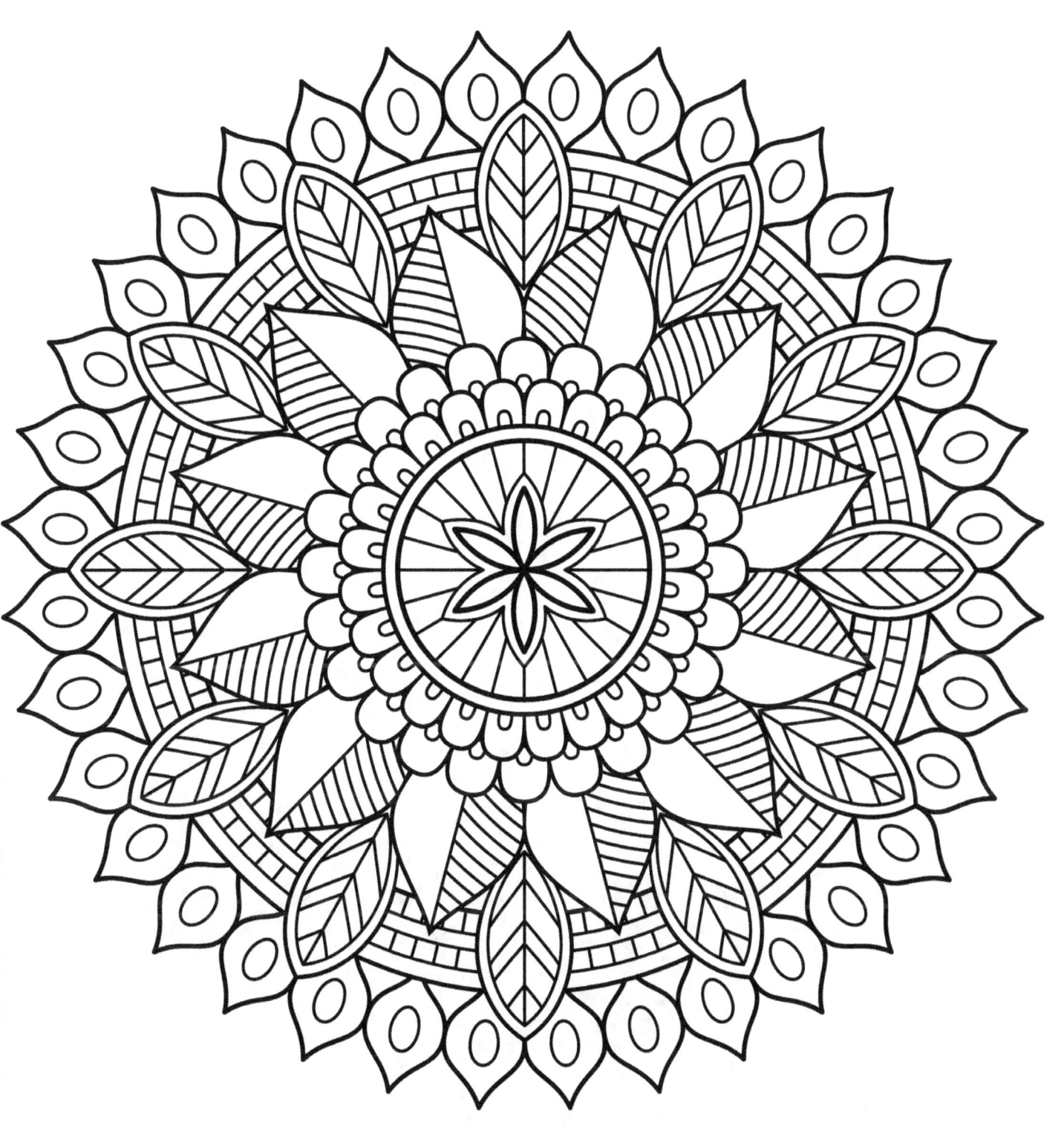

_____

___ / ___ / ___

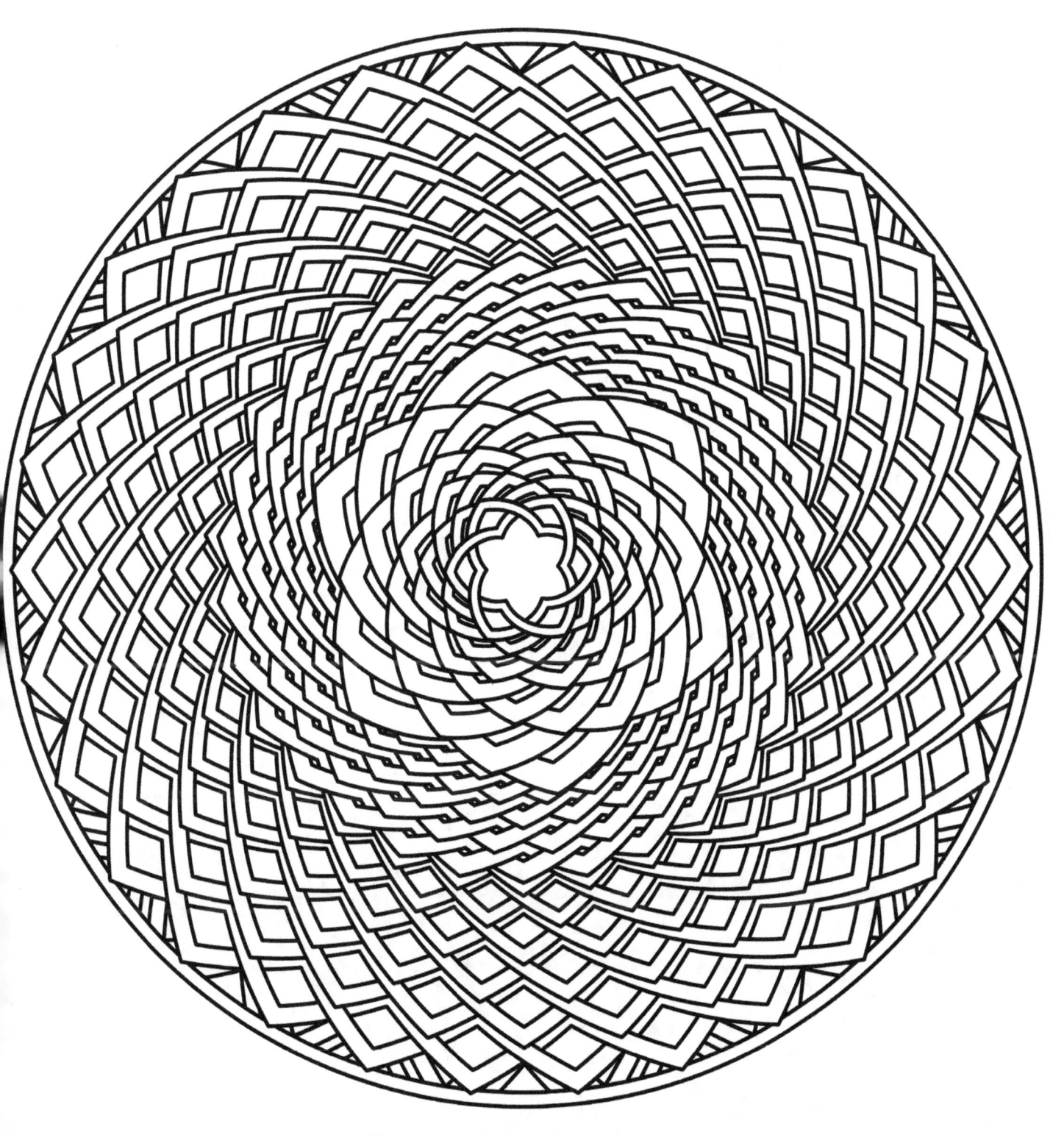

_____

___ / ___ / ___

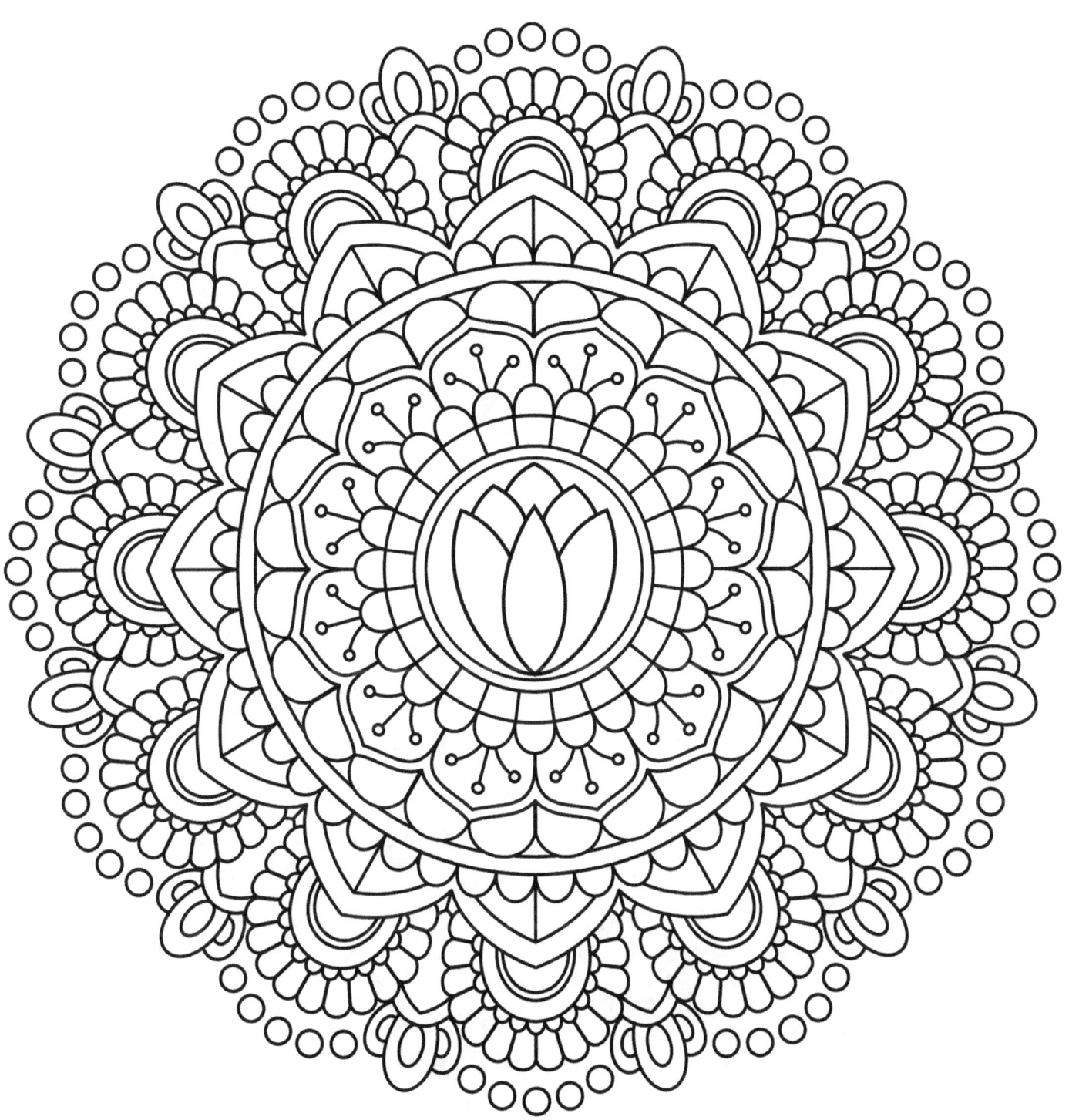

_____

___ / ___ / ___

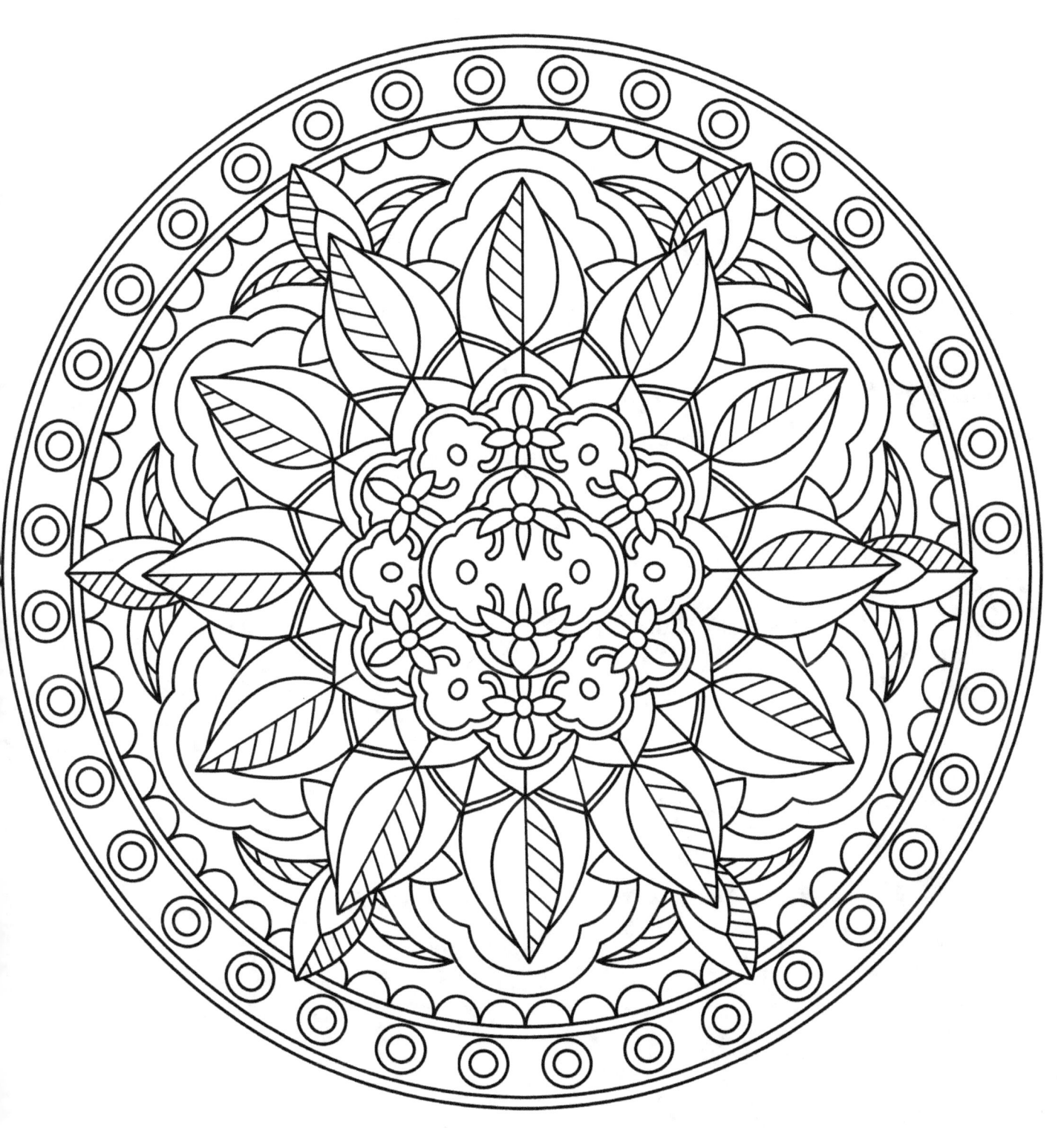

___/___/___

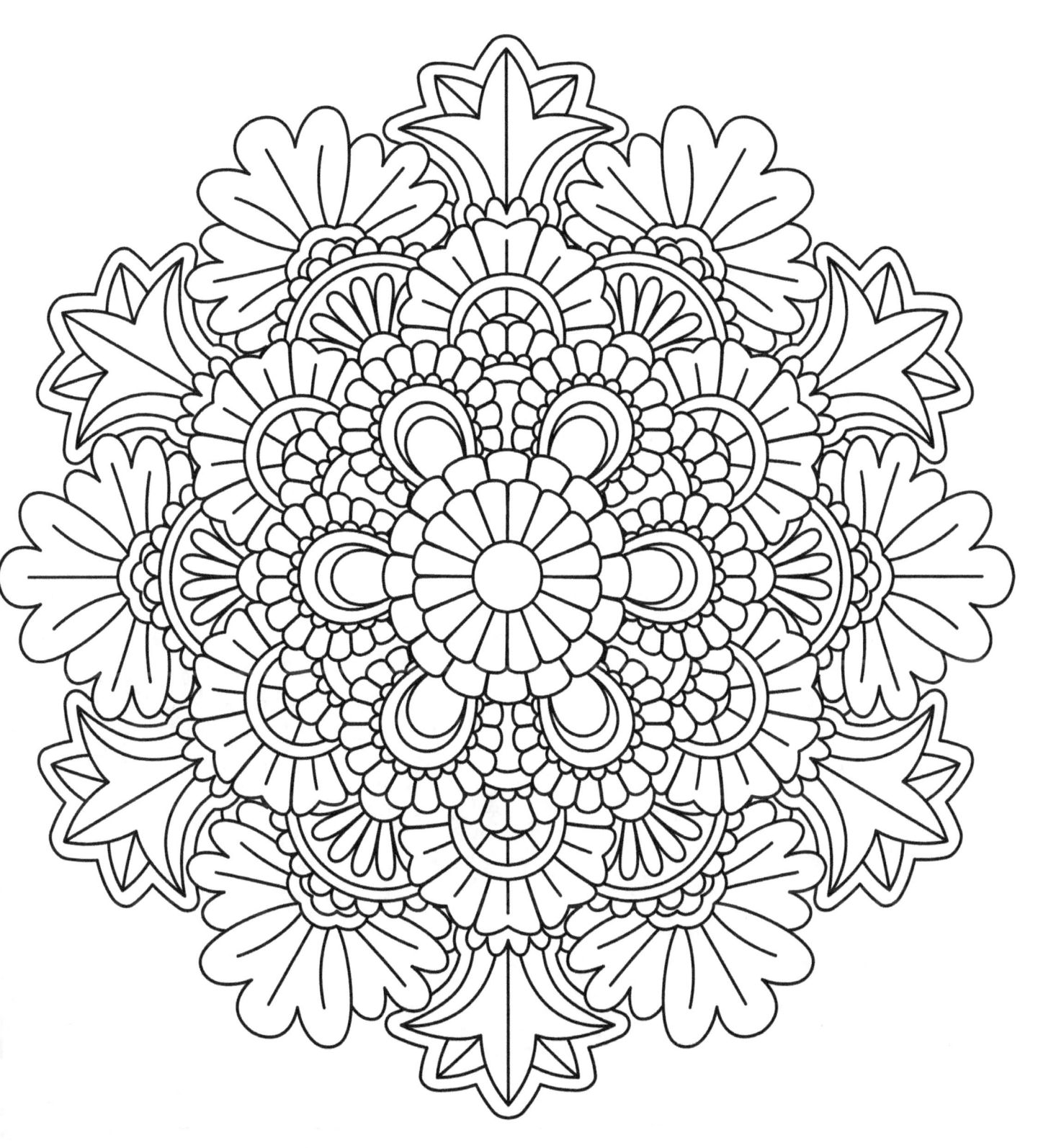

___/___/___

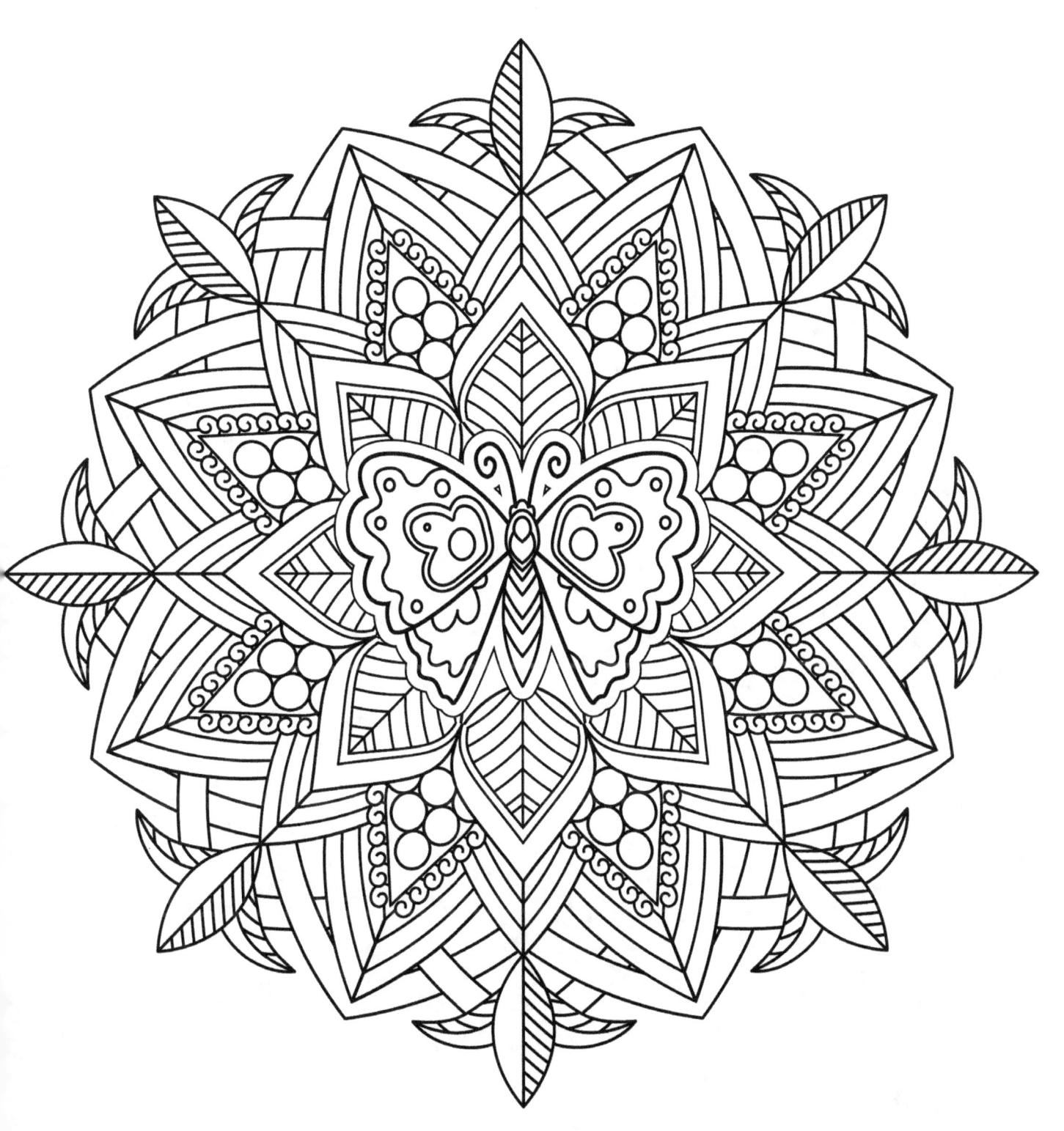

_____

___ / ___ / ___

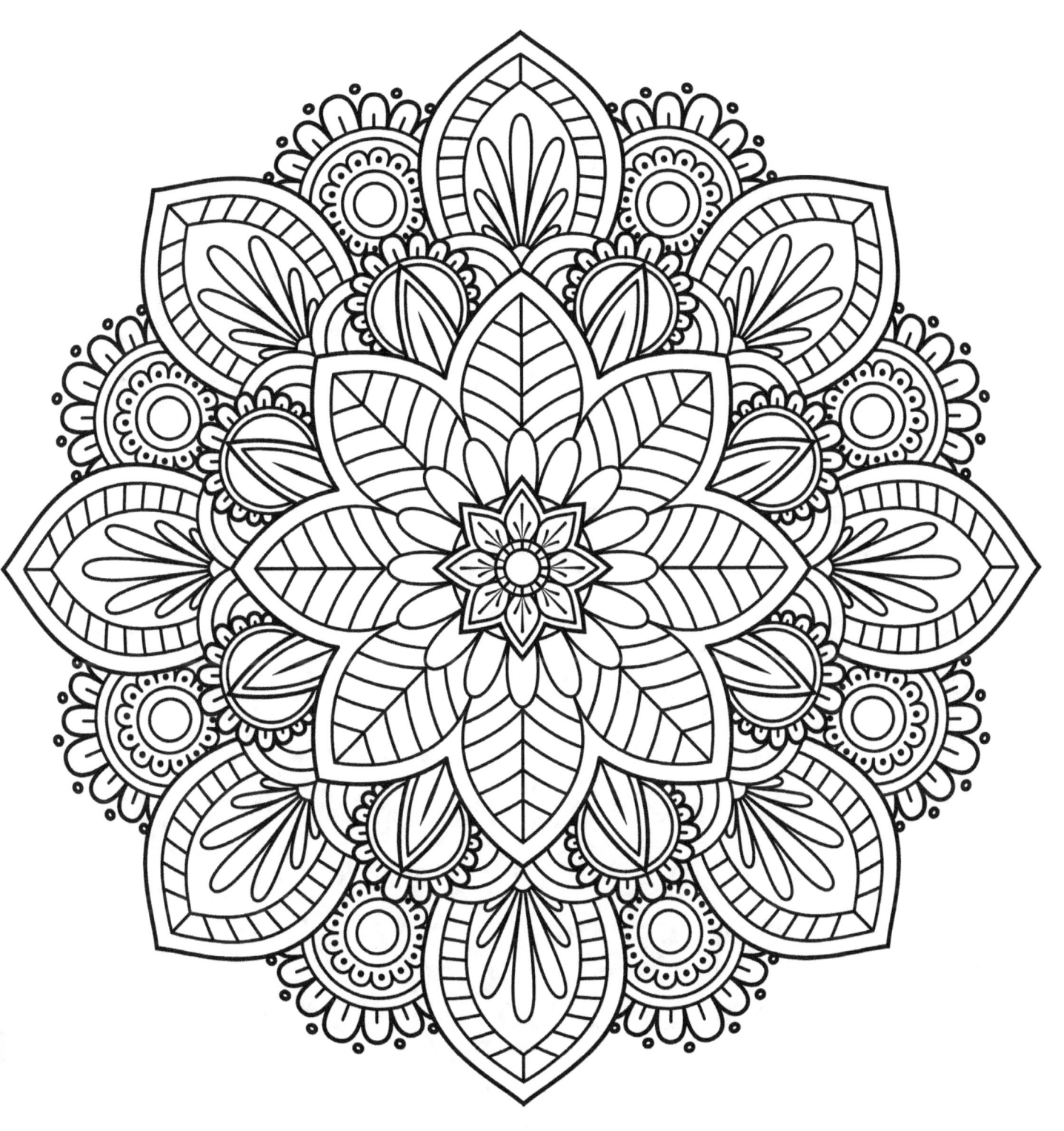

——— / ——— / ———

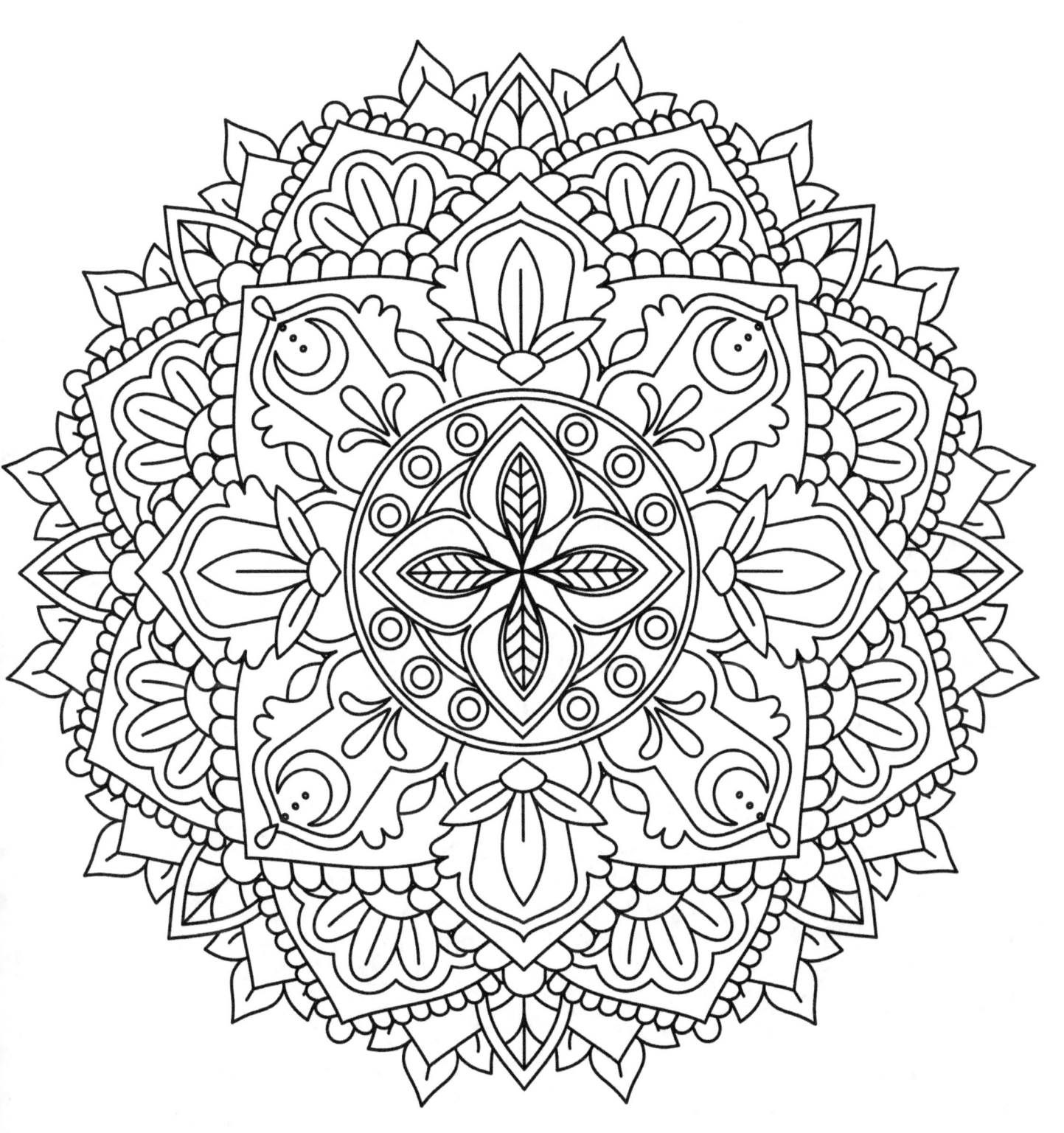

_____

___ / ___ / ___

THE END

OR IS IT ?

The following pages are examples of up coming coloring books I am working on.

To be notified on new books and pages signup at

https://colorbyaj.com/signup

INTRICATE MANDALAS VOL 1

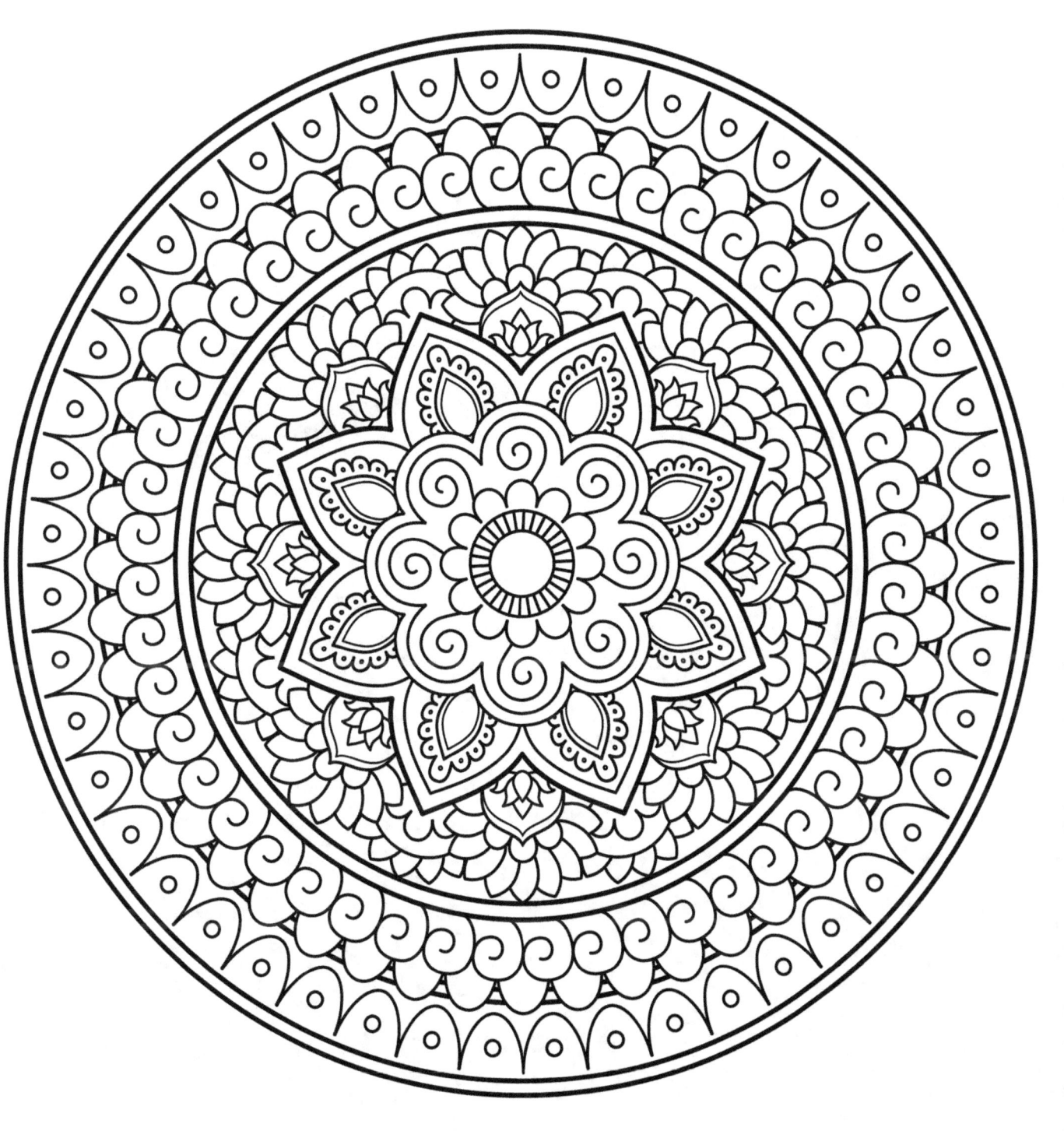

INTRICATE MANDALAS VOL 1

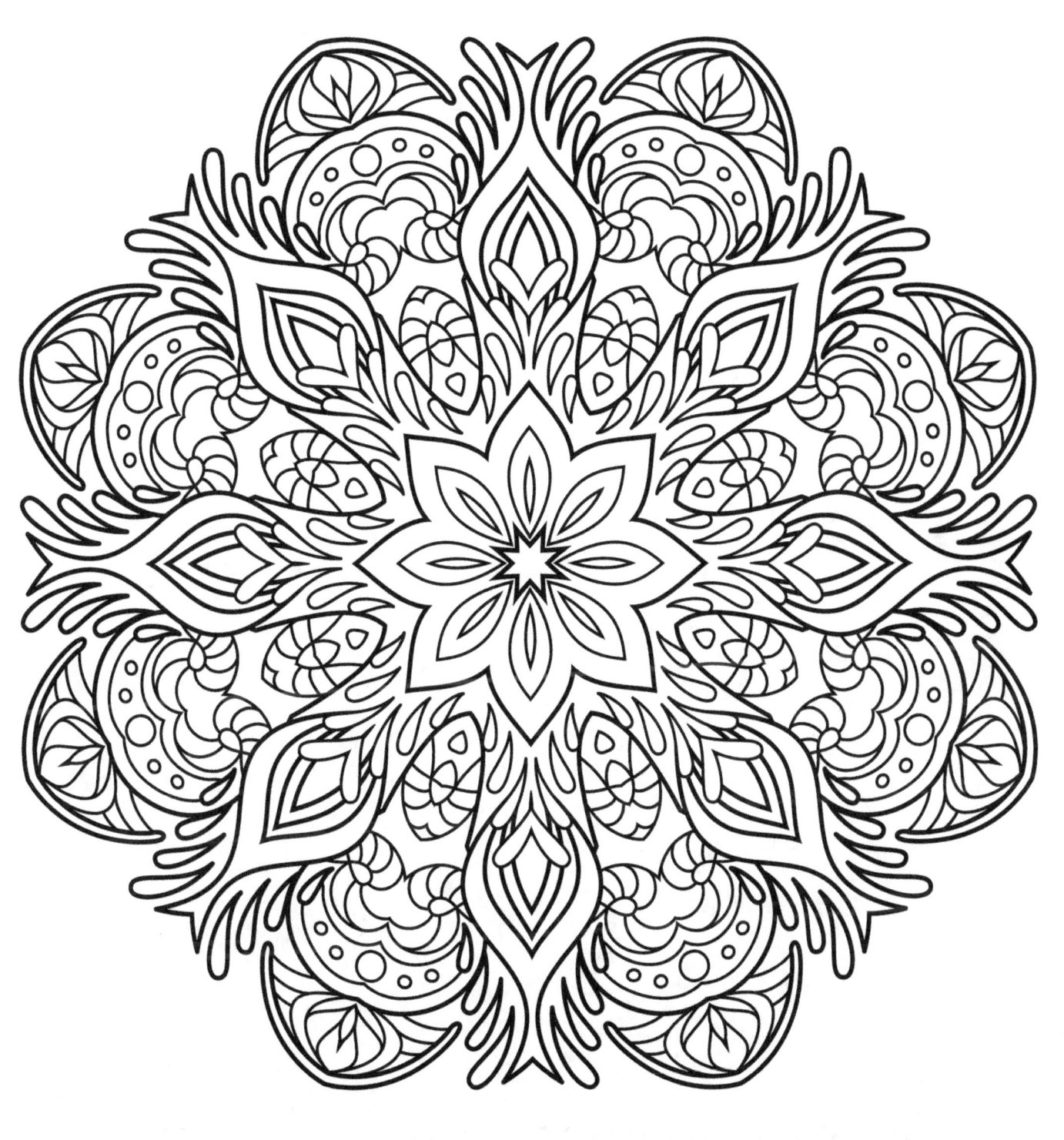

MINDFUL MANDALAS VOL 2

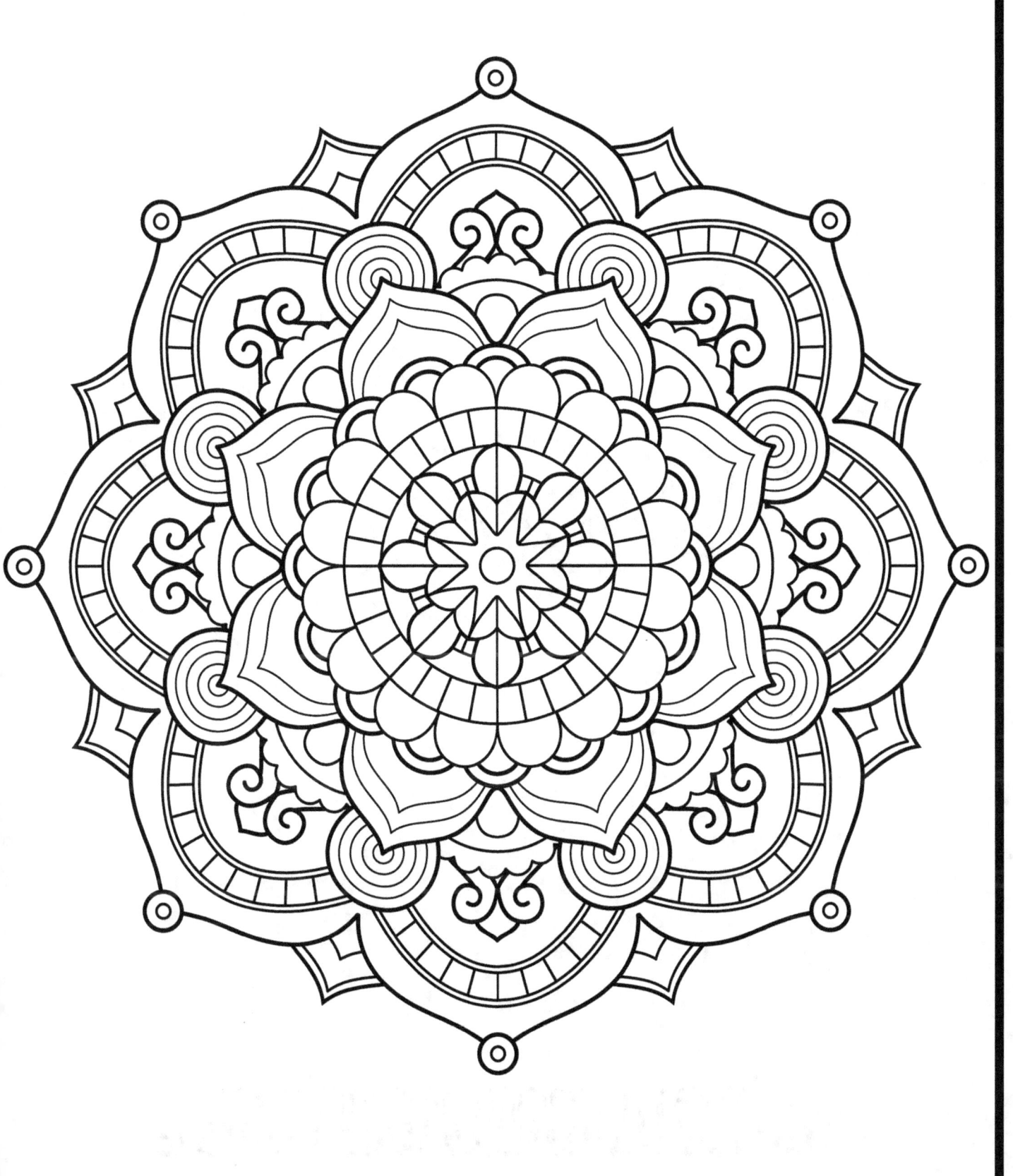

MINDFUL MANDALAS VOL 2

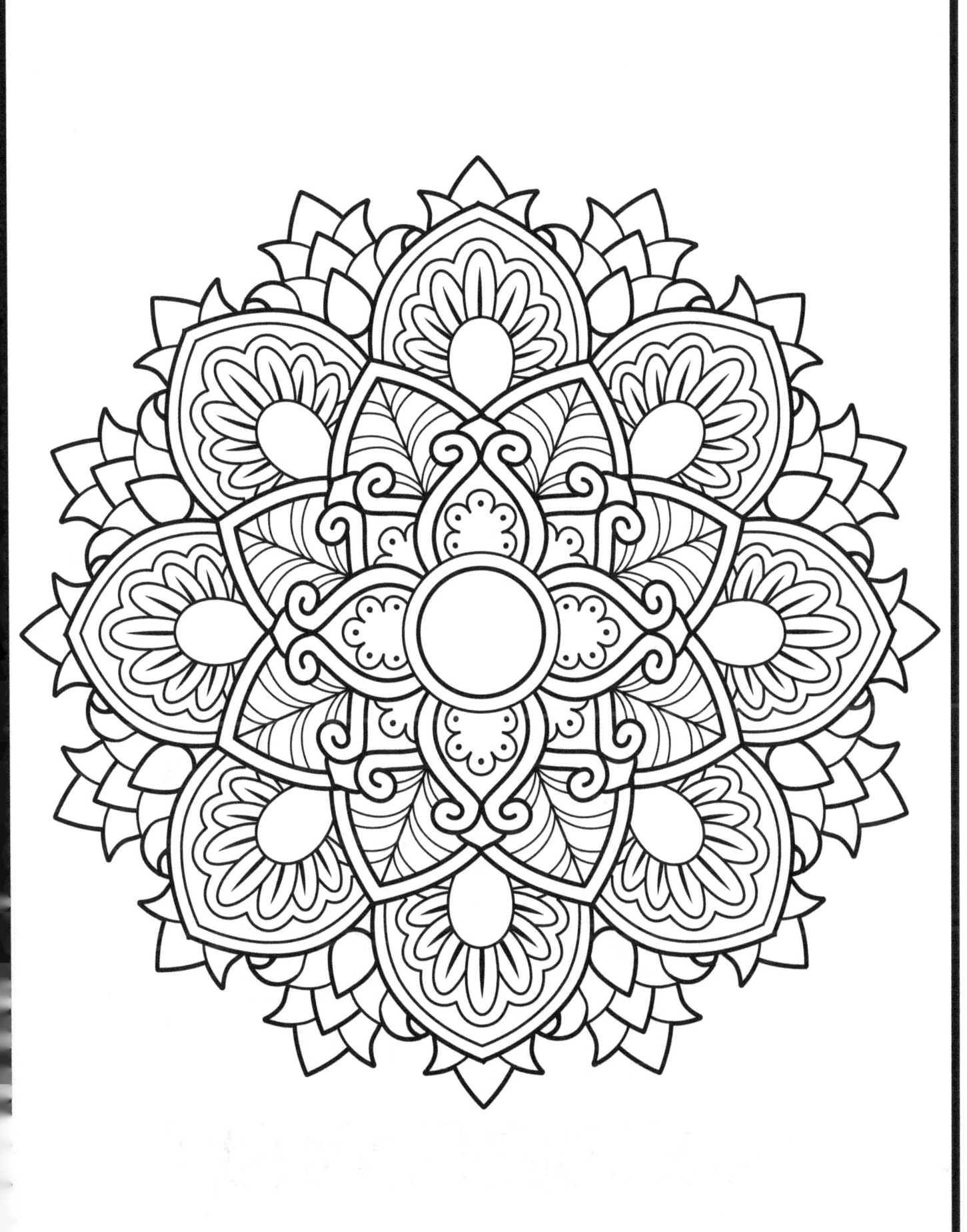

RELAXING PATTERNS VOL 1

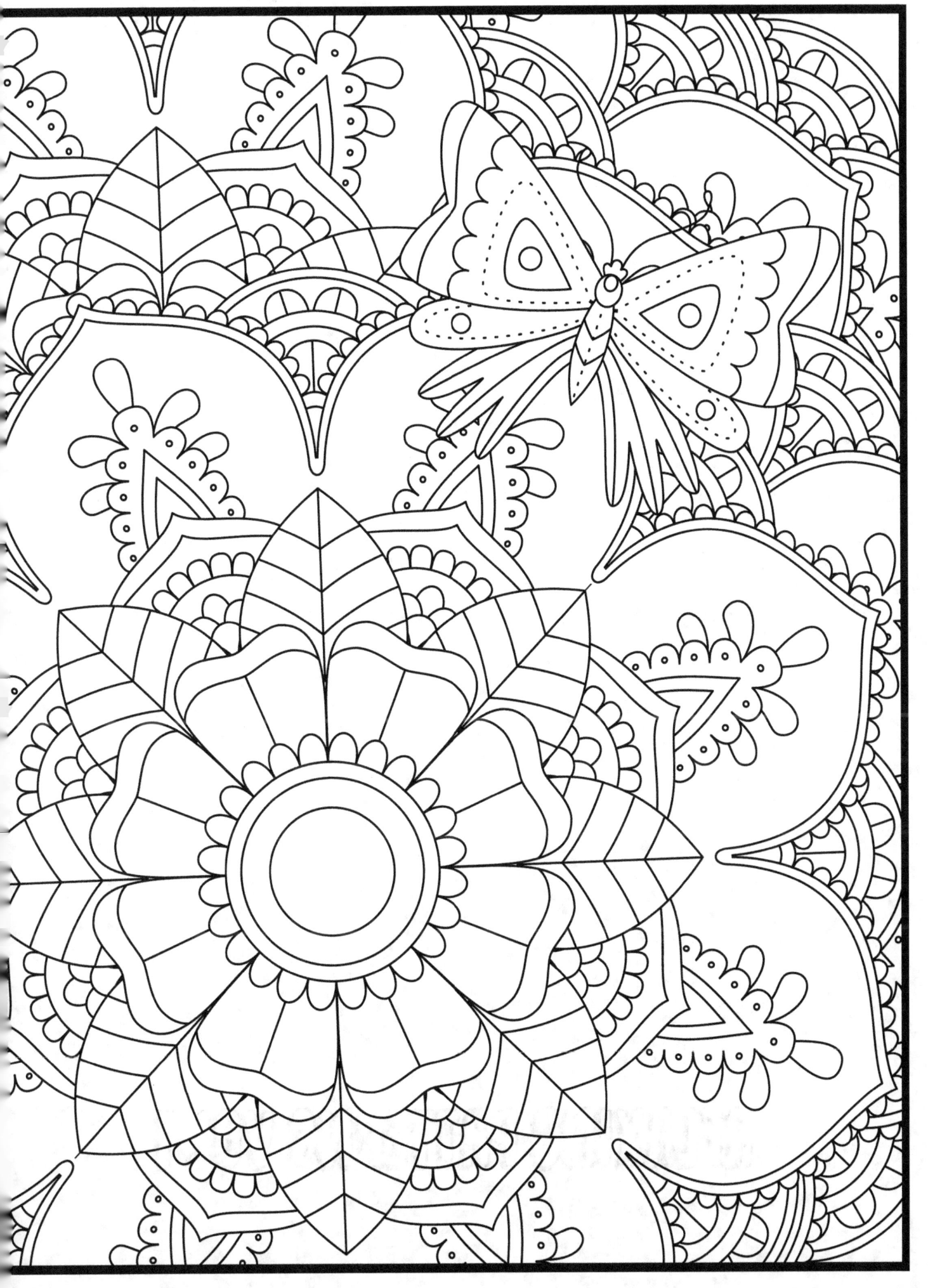

RELAXING PATTERNS VOL 1

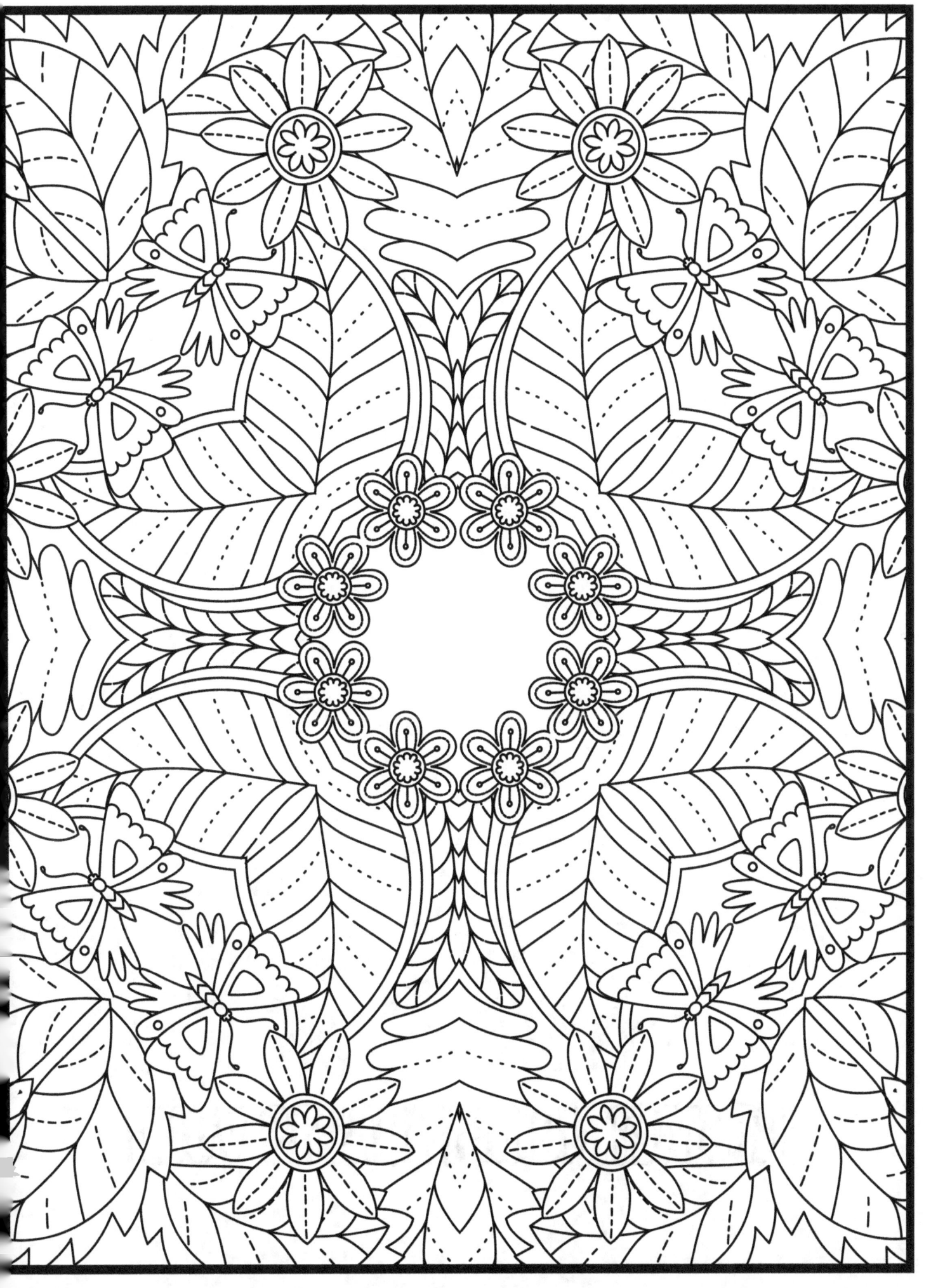

GEOMETRIC MANDALAS VOL 1

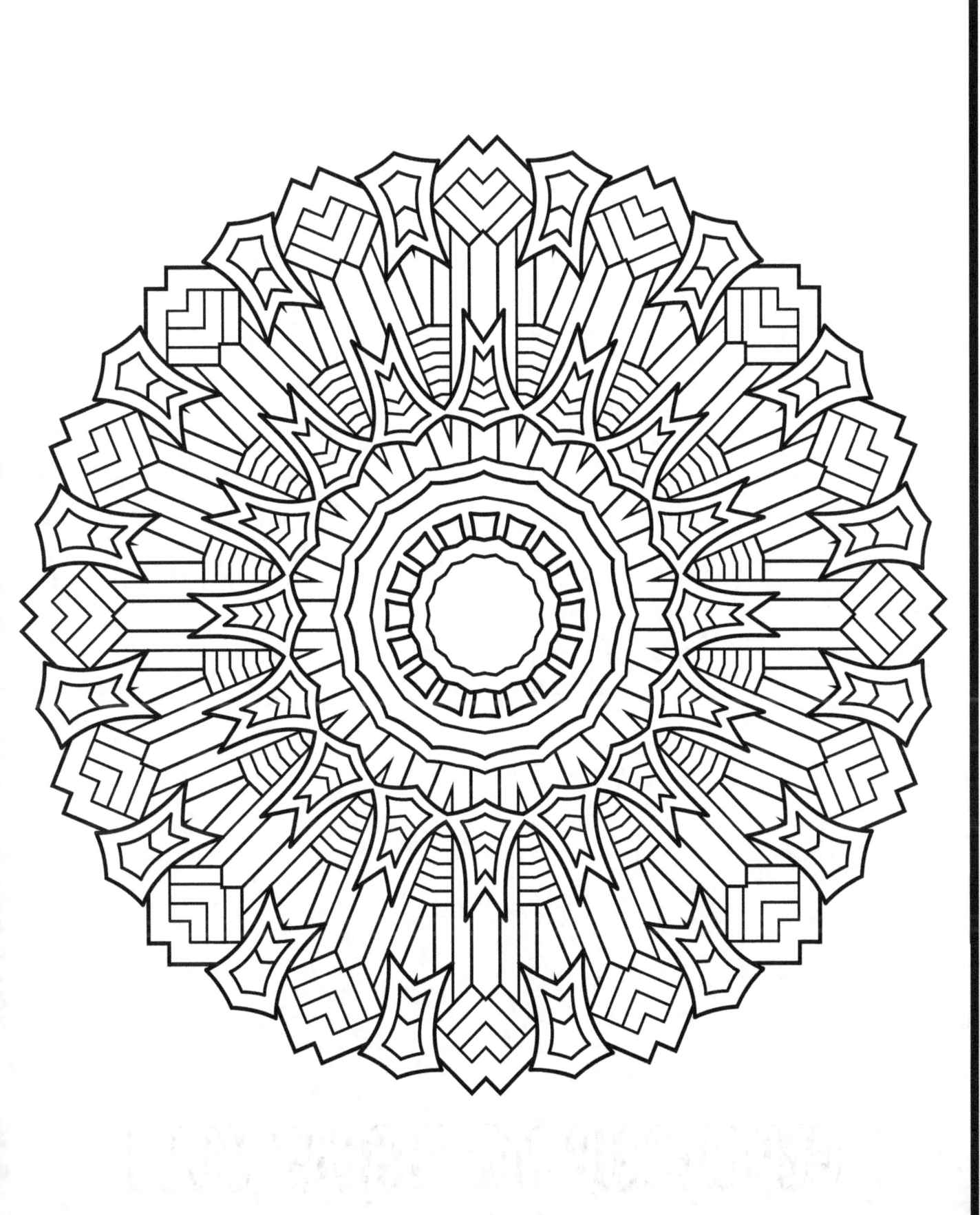

GEOMETRIC MANDALAS VOL 1

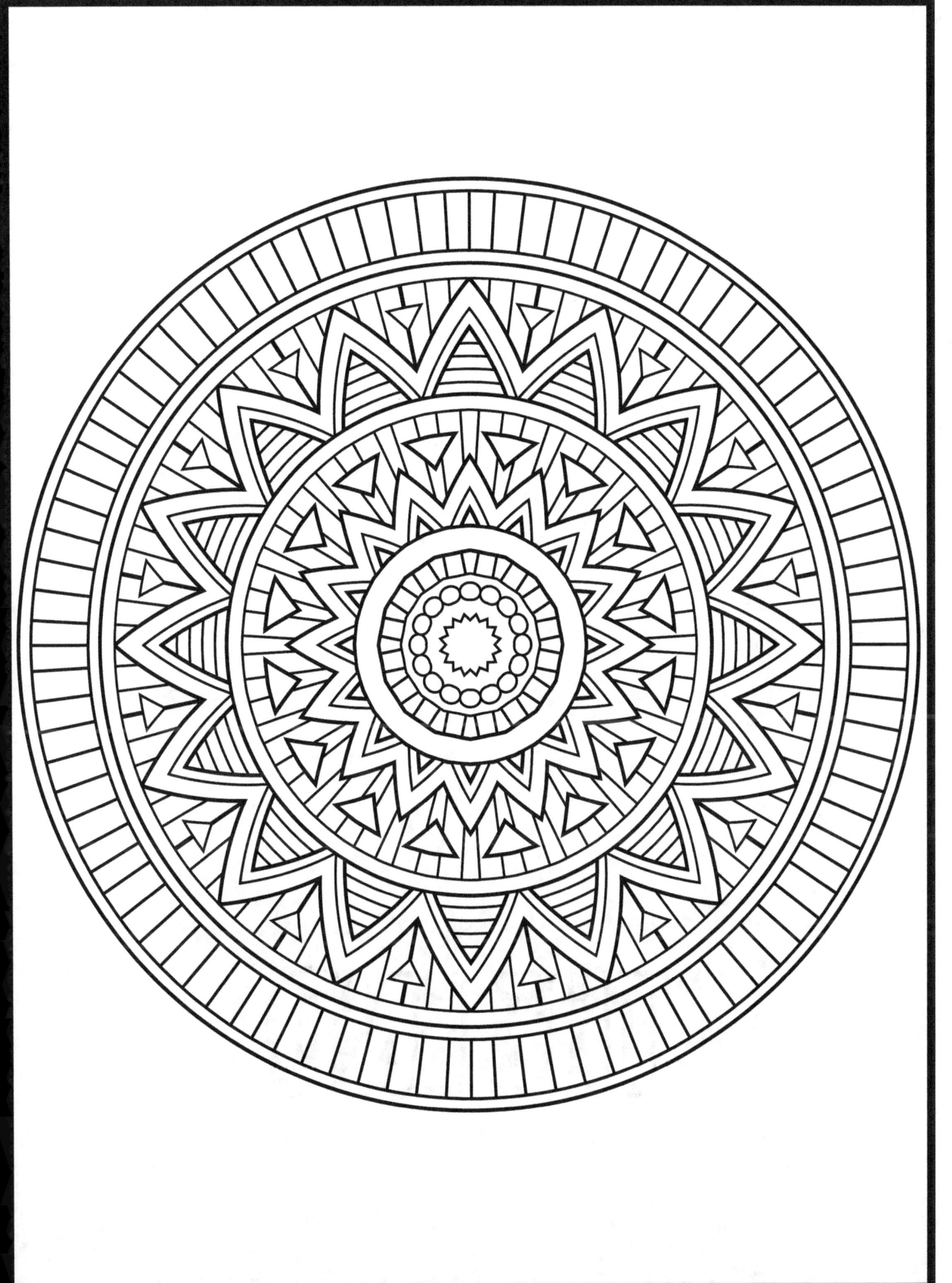

THE END

I hoped you enjoyed this coloring experience?

If you did, can I ask you for a small favor in the form of a honest review.
It doesn't have to be long, just a sentence would be appreciated, thank you.

Here is a direct link..

colorbyaj.com/mindful

Many thanks, Aj

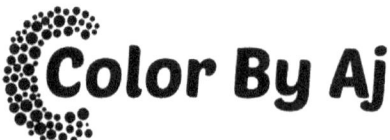

MINDFUL mandalas

Relaxing Adult Coloring Book Volume 1 - Improved Edition

Color Test Page

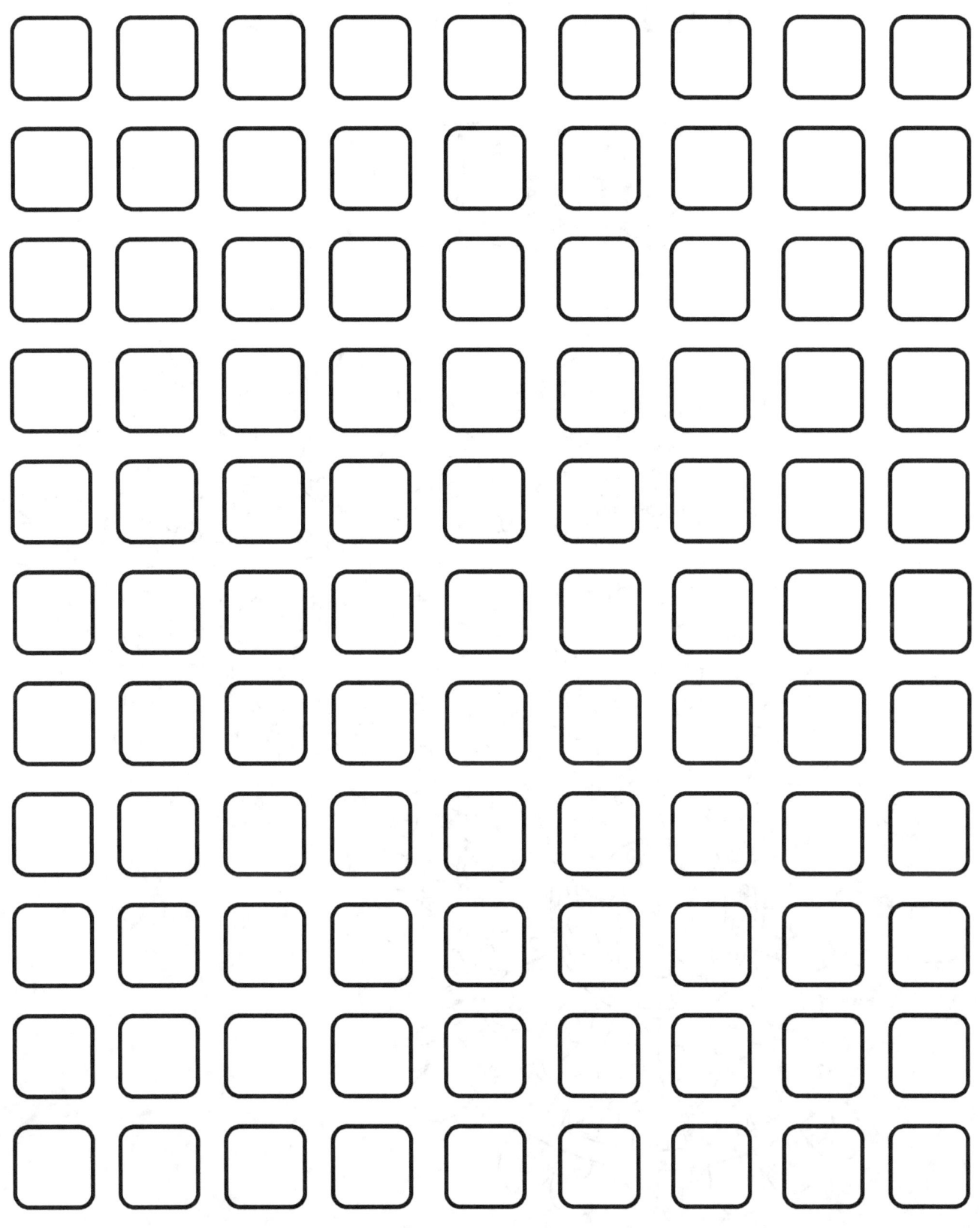

PRACTICE SHEET

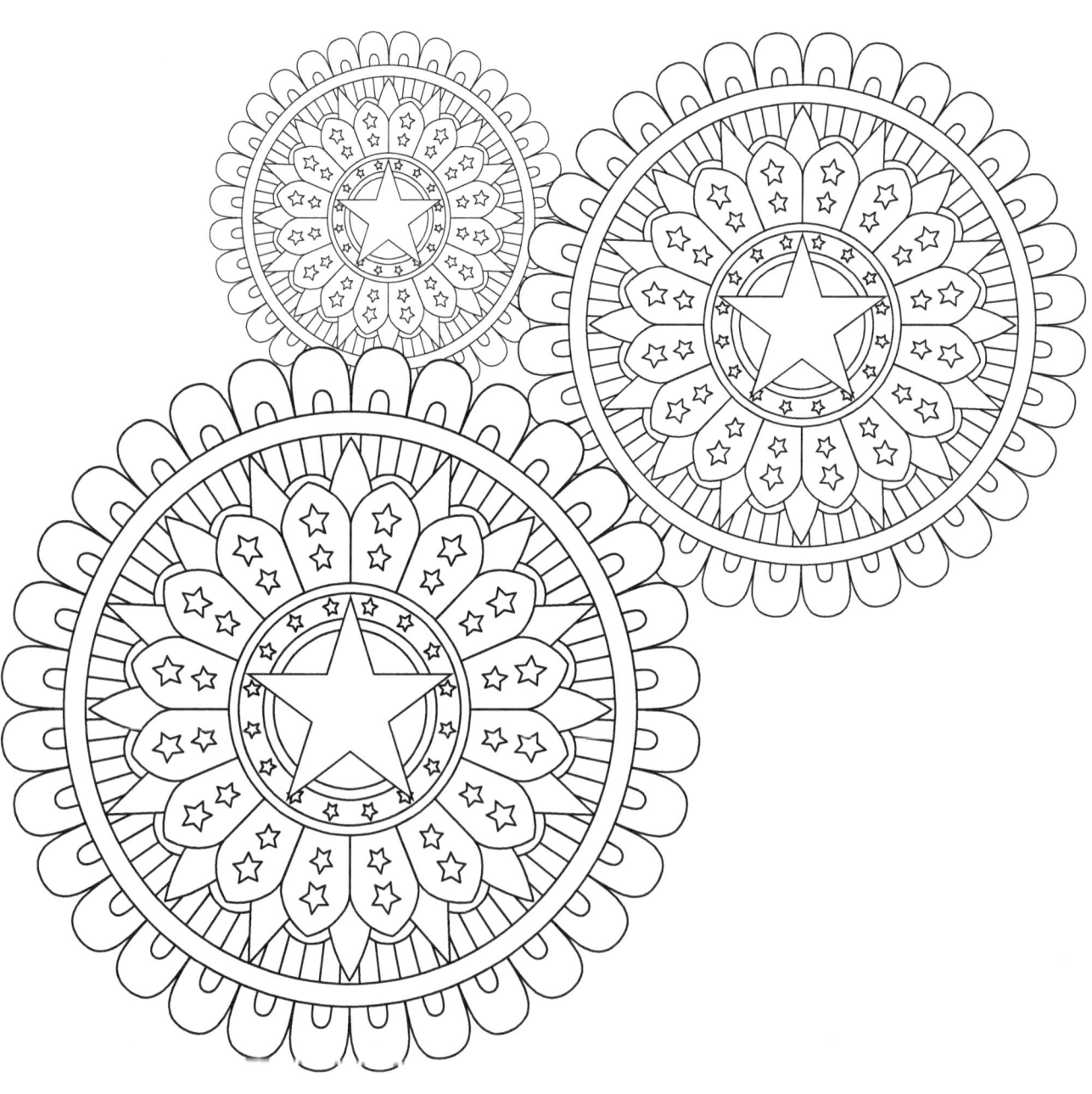

BLOTTER SHEET

Cut this sheet out with an Exacto blade and use this behind the page you are coloring to help prevent bleed through.

Adult Coloring Book with
30 Mindful Mandala Designs to Color

By AJBailey
Copyright © 2020 AJ Bailey. All rights reserved
Website: colorbyaj.com

www.ingramcontent.com/pod-product-compliance
Lightning Source LLC
Chambersburg PA
CBHW080514220526
45465CB00006B/2484